Encountered

in

Worship

**An Expression of
the Heart**

Dean Maerz

Copyright Information

Published By:

Creative Launch Publishing

Abbotsford, BC, Canada

www.mycreativelaunch.com

cl CREATIVE LAUNCH

Scripture Quotation Permissions

Table of Contents

ACKNOWLEDGMENTS

There are many people who have encouraged me along the pathway of this project. Prayer is vital when writing, especially when the subject is personal and close to the heart. To those who have prayed—Karitas and Nathan Townsend, Christine Foth, Cathy Lee, and my wife, Adeline, thank you.

Editing is also crucial and this book has been through a few different refinement phases. Thank you to Misty Bedwell for coaxing me through the first round. You forced me to think outside the box and gave me the courage to explore ideas far beyond where I would have gone on my own. Thanks also to Carolyn Currey for your second round copyediting and proofing super-skills. You helped me rethink, refocus, and reword. Your attention to detail is outstanding— nothing escapes your notice.

I would also like to thank the two of you for your contributions to the last chapter. I appreciate it more than you will ever know.

To all of the test readers, thank you for taking the time, and for your comments and feedback.

And finally, to my Lord Jesus—the one who is worthy of all glory, honor, praise, and worship. None of this makes any sense without you. There are not words enough to say thank you

DEDICATION

This book is dedicated to all the worshipers I have been privileged to cross paths with over the years. You have come in many different ages, giftings, and ethnicities.

To all my friends who are singers, instrumentalists, worship leaders, dancers, artists, writers, recording artists, graphic artists, dramatic actors, banner wavers, makeup artists, photographers, costume makers, stage directors, sound and lighting technicians, and choreographers—this is for you. While writing this manuscript, you have been a constant source of inspiration, never far from my mind and heart.

I look forward to worshiping together with you for eternity.

FOREWORD

(by Steve Schroeder)

The greatest desire of the Father is to give Himself fully to us. Our response to this gift is to worship.

I came across a magazine article on worship written years ago by someone I have always received insight and life from. In the article he wrote:

"To worship or not to worship has never been the question. For all God's created beings are inherently worshipers. Heaven is full of worship. It's the stuff of which heaven is made. The book of Revelation progressively shows worship being performed by every inhabitant of heaven including mankind. No matter how vociferously they may deny it, each person on earth is a worshiper. It is in their genetic strain."

I am a worshiper. Not merely a worshiper, but a worshiper first. Something happens in my innermost being that magnetically draws me into alignment with the Father's heart when I worship. It is as though my spirit becomes unbound to this world and is swept up in union with all of heaven.

Let me illustrate with a story.

After receiving some news that troubled ours hearts, we headed to the house of some dear friends for dinner. Our friends are worshipers. Years before, we used to live next door to them as families. I recall hearing their grand piano pounding out worship in the early mornings—music that resounded through the walls into our home. It brought a smile to our faces whenever we heard it.

We worry, He dances

We had just enjoyed a great dinner and conversation together when our host asked if we wanted to head into the living room and worship. The words leapt out of my mouth "Dinner was great, but we really came to worship."

From the moment the first note was struck, I was transported into the presence of the Father. As I was there, beholding the throne, I had a picture of Jesus dressed in a plain, long garment that flowed easily as He moved. He began to dance to our worship. As He danced, He started to spin, head swung back, breaking out into laughter full of joy. As He spun, I caught His huge, great smile.

I watched Him closely as He danced effortlessly. Then, suddenly, He glanced over his shoulder at me and said, *"Hey Steve, you worry, I DANCE!"*

With these words, I began to weep, not with sorrow, but with a surprising lightness that instantly unbound me from the burden I was carrying. It was a remarkable experience— I worshiped with tears of freedom that day. To think that His dancing broke the chains that the enemy attempted to shackle me with is incredible. It gives us insight into His nature and the power of worship. All I could think about for days were His words: "You worry, I dance."

One encounter in worship will change your life.

Dean is my friend. We have a kindred spirit. We are both worshipers and we love the presence of the Father more than anything. Something profound happens when you encounter the Father in worship. It compels you to share the experience with others in the hope that it might stir in them the same longing to be fully unbound and alive in Him.

It has been said that a shared joy is twice a joy. This is the desire and reality of the words and stories written in the pages of this book. I am honored to walk with Dean and to encourage you, along with him, into the realm of the profound and powerful—into an invitation to be encountered. Encountered in worship.

It has stirred in me a renewed hunger for more. It will in you as well.

Steve Schroeder "Uncle Steve"

President CMA

Christian Ministers Association Canada

PREFACE

A few months ago, my wife and I held a small dinner party at our house. We invited a couple over whom we hadn't seen in a few years—worship leaders at a church that we had previously worked for. We had been in a life group together for a period of time and I also had the honor of dedicating their first baby to the Lord.

Grant and Cathy hadn't stepped two inches inside our door before I noticed something different about them. They were both beaming from ear to ear and the glory of God was radiant all over them. I knew immediately that they had been spending time in God's presence—they were wrecked!

We had a great time catching up that evening. We talked about Jesus, His presence, worship, the glory of God, and the prophetic—my favorite subjects! They told us how God had led them to a new church where they had become directors of worship. Cathy, in particular, told us many stories—how

Jesus had opened up the eyes of her heart and showed her numerous pictures and dreams. It was humbling to see the transformation that had taken place in their lives.

Just before they were getting ready to leave, we decided to pray together. As we did, Cathy looked at me and sputtered rather awkwardly, "I have a gift for you tonight from Jesus that is, in the end, for my own benefit. But I can't receive it unless I give it to you first. Would you like it?"

I replied that I was open to whatever she had for me.

She got up and boldly headed for our pantry. After fumbling around for a minute, she reappeared with some olive oil and stood in front of me as I sat on the couch. After smearing oil on my forehead, she touched my lips with her oil soaked finger. She then asked me to stretch out both of my hands and she proceeded to anoint each one of my fingers. After praying a blessing over me, she told me what the gift was—I was to write!

Immediately I knew I had been set up. Writing is not new to me, but I really did not want this project. Jesus had been prompting me to write a book on worship for months already. I kept protesting, telling Him that there was really nothing more to say on the subject.

With so many readily available worship resources, I couldn't imagine writing a whole book full of fresh, anointed material, but in that moment, I determined to be obedient. I also struck up a deal with Cathy that I would only write if she prayed for me during the entire process, something she did faithfully.

As I started in on this book, the Holy Spirit clearly impressed on my heart that I was to be in a place of worship and presence throughout the entire writing process. At times, when I tried to get into a creative space without it, there was absolutely no inspiration. When I put on worship music and took the time to enter God's presence, the words flowed easily and naturally. This entire manuscript has been written in the atmosphere of heaven.

And so, to my sister Cathy, here is your gift—from Jesus, to you, to me, and now back to you again. I pray that you are encountered by glory as you read it, even more than I was in writing it.

Your brother,

Dean

Chapter 1

THE JOURNEY BEGINS

It was a hot, Sunday afternoon in the middle of July. My wife and I had been invited, along with a group of young adults, to lead worship at a small Vineyard church in our downtown core. After hauling our sound equipment up two huge flights of stairs, we began the set-up process. Each person had a specific task. Some were in charge of plugging in cables. Others were setting up speakers and amps.

Our keyboard player was wearing rather tight black jeans. When she bent down to adjust her keyboard stand, a critical seam split open and so she was frantically running around trying to find a needle and some thread. There were always plenty of laughs to be had with this bunch! We finally finished our setup, did our sound check, and retired to a small, muggy room to pray before the service started.

Sunday evening church began and we launched into our song list. There were maybe forty or fifty people in attendance but in true Vineyard fashion, they worshiped with all their hearts. As we began playing our third song, the presence of God was already starting to fill the room. We were used to lingering musically when these junctures came along, so we began to play spontaneously, eventually building up to a big song bridge. It was at this moment I witnessed one of the funniest things I have ever seen in my life.

A young man, possibly in his early twenties, got inspired and grabbed a flag that was in a holder beside the stage. He then began to run barefoot around the perimeter of the small, dusty, hardwood floor room—flag billowing straight out behind him. He circled the room twice, then rounded the corner of the middle aisle, and headed for the front of the room.

In my mind, everything from this moment onward seemed to move in slow motion. With eyes closed and heart completely absorbed in worship, our friend sprinted down the aisle with all the poise of an Olympic athlete carrying a flag for his country. When he finally opened his eyes, he was too close to the front of the room to make what needed to be a tight turn. A look of sudden terror seized him as he tried to stop but it was too late. His bare feet lost their grip on the dusty floor and he went sprawling onto the small stage area. His flag flew out of his hands, striking our worship leader squarely across the face, knocking his trendy glasses onto the floor.

> *Worship is not a career to me, it is a calling*

After wiping out our second guitar player's pedal board, our flag carrying friend's ill-fated journey finally came to an end about six inches in front of my feet. Our big bridge just kind of ended—almost with a similar sound effect to pulling an electrical plug out of a wall socket. At first, we were all in shock. Then shock gave way to hysteria to the point where it was difficult to continue on with any kind of worship whatsoever. Oh, the sense of humor our God has!

Even though this incident stands out as unique, it is only one of a countless number of worship services I have been involved in over my lifetime. Worship is not a career to me. It is a calling.

My journey with worship started even before I was born. My mother would rest her accordion on top of my still developing, prenatal head and play for hours. She would also pray for me, dedicating me to the work of the house of God in a similar fashion to Samuel's mother, Hannah.

As a child, I found myself in regular attendance, sitting on the wooden pews of our country church. We sang with only a piano on one side of the platform and an organ on the other side for accompaniment.

I started to learn to play the piano at the age of seven. The following year, I began to learn how to play the bass guitar using an instrument that my dad handmade. When I was nine years old, my parents bought me a drum set—a bold move in a time when drums weren't even allowed in the church. A couple of years later I bought my first guitar. Learning and mastering these instruments came easily and naturally to me.

As I entered my teens, I began attending various youth services. I have vivid memories of our Wednesday night youth group. We would sing with sincere hearts using a guitar for accompaniment. During these years there was little in the way of Christian music and those bands that did play were not considered worship bands—they were called Christian rock bands. There were ongoing arguments in our rural community church over these issues as new generations struggled to find meaning and relevant worship that fit their culture.

During my later teens, my parents began hosting a home church in the living room of our house. There were fifteen or twenty people who attended. We sang and prayed together for hours and at times the Holy Spirit would descend on our gatherings. These adventures deepened my understanding of worship.

One Friday evening, our family went into the city for a revival meeting. At the end of the service, all of the youth were called forward and organized into a long line. I didn't know it then, but I was about to have my first experience with a "fire tunnel." Someone laid their hands on me and I went out under the power of God. A few minutes later, I regained consciousness on the floor. I was enveloped in warmth and light from head to toe, and it took me a while before I could even move. It was my first significant encounter with the presence of God and I was never the same afterwards. It was as if I was a marked person, like someone had put a seal on my heart. I now realize that the Holy Spirit touched my life, setting me aside for His work.

After I graduated from high school, I joined an international music-based missions ministry. I traveled with this organization for a few years and it was here that I first became aware of praise. Up until this time, we would sing but it wasn't considered praise or worship. It was called the "song service." However, the founder of our missions group had learned that there was tremendous power in bringing praise to the streets of the darkest places of our world.

Our adventures involved setting up our sound system in outdoor squares, schools, theaters, and various other locations. There we exalted the name of Jesus with our music. The results were profound. Most people had never felt the sense of God's presence that fills a space when praise is released. This experience would leave them undone and they would often turn their hearts over to Jesus when given an invitation to do so.

Once I left this organization, I became part of a church music staff under a pastor who had a clear understanding of what it meant to worship. We would worship for hours, especially on Sunday evenings with no time restraint or agenda. It was here that a lifelong hunger for God's presence ignited in

> *A lifelong hunger for God's presence ignited in me*

me. I began to long for the presence in personal as well as corporate times of worship. I remember Sunday evenings when the glory of God was so strong, we could barely stand.

I eventually moved on to work for another church, and it was here that my story took on an interesting twist. A close family member had just graduated from high school and was looking for a place to rent as he launched out into the work world. Our pastor and his wife had an empty suite in their basement and so he moved in with them.

In a few short months, what seemed like an innocent relocation on his part turned into a heartbreaking ordeal. He quickly became embroiled in a situation beset with sexual indiscretion, deception, and moral failure beyond comprehension.

These things soon affected my wife and I, throwing our hearts into turmoil. We became conflicted and confused as we tried to navigate the murkiest of waters. Involved in the darkness were trusted leaders and pastors who had become close personal friends.

People who have never worked for a church might not realize that a church job is different from any other type of employment that exists. Every part of life is involved. It is your source of income. It is also your church, your spiritual family, your friends, and your community. Authority lines often become blurred as pastors and trusted mentors play a dual role as employment supervisors. It also carries a deep sense of connection to God and His purpose for your life.

To add to these factors, I was idealistic and my identity was dangerously linked to my job. All of these things created a recipe for disaster, and disaster struck me hard. After a little more than a year at this church, my worship directing duties came to an unceremonious end. All of the "eggs" in my life were in one basket and when the basket fell, the eggs all broke at once. Everything I loved was terminated in the span of a day. My family was broken beyond description, my job was gone, my friends were ripped out of my life, and my sense of destiny was shattered.

I was hurt beyond measure and cried for several days straight. Then, after about a week, my heart completely shut down. I foolishly and proudly declared that I would never work for a church again and I spent the next several years of my life wandering—first unemployed, then going from menial job to job, playing music in bars and pubs for extra money. I became bitter, cynical, chronically sick, and clinically depressed for almost ten years.

Since my entire life had been music, I eventually took on a full roster of music students, teaching them week-to-week. During this time, a very strange thing happened. Though I deliberately kept a great distance from any church, I began to get dozens of Christian guitar students. To my horror, the kind of music they wanted to learn to play was worship music. Each time I listened to one of their songs, I was agitated to no end. I often woke up in the middle of the night with their worship tunes stuck in my mind, like a playlist with no stop button.

Then something else happened. About a half hour from where we lived, there was a large gathering every Sunday night consisting of nothing more than a band leading worship for nearly two hours. My students began telling me about these services and persistently inviting me to come— an invitation that I turned down countless times.

I clearly remember the first time I gave in and headed out to this gathering. Well, I remember the first few minutes of what happened. I recall proudly striding into the large auditorium, finding a seat, checking out the band and the sound system, and then the rest is a blank for me. I only know that for the next two hours, I was weeping like a baby. Almost a decade of bitterness and hurt came gushing out of me as the presence of God, released in worship, sovereignly apprehended me. It seemed to wash over me in wave after wave. By the end of the night, I was exhausted beyond measure. The next morning, when I woke up, I knew that something insanely good had happened inside of me.

A few nights later, my healing journey continued with a vivid prophetic dream. I was looking at a church calendar printed on a pink piece of "8.5 x 11" paper. It had a grid with the days of the month and all the church activities were written on the different days. I began protesting that nothing on it really made a difference in anybody's life, and declaring that it was all culturally irrelevant.

The next thing I knew, I was out of my body and floating. I could see my wife and myself sound asleep on our bed and I seemed to be looking from behind the headboard—as if through the wall. Then I saw the most stunning thing. Two angels entered the room and stood facing my side of the bed. I had never seen an angel before and these two creatures were magnificent. I was looking at their profiles from the side. They had their heads bowed, and their long hair was hanging down from the

> *For the first time in years I could feel again*

sides of their heads, concealing their faces. One of them had dark hair and the other one was more blonde. They had gold headbands and golden sashes on their robes. I remember noting the remarkable contrast between their extremely white robes and the skin of their arms, which was almost glowing like bronze.

At this point, one of the angels reached down and touched me slowly and deliberately five times. Each time he touched me, I screamed out in extreme pain! But each time, the pain decreased slightly until the fifth time, when it was all but gone. The next morning, once again, I knew something profound had happened in my heart. For the first time in years, I could feel again! I began to realize that I had been brought face to face with nothing less than pure and amazing grace.

In the days that followed, I began to come alive again. In my years of bitterness, you could have preached a thousand sermons at me on the subject of forgiveness and my heart would not have responded to one of them. One encounter with Jesus changed all of that. I found a new strength to forgive and learned that forgiveness was a decision—first minute-by-minute, then hourly, then daily, weekly, monthly, yearly, and finally for the rest of my life.

My wife and I gradually began going back to church. I also started taking my guitar into a quiet room and worshiping for as long as I could spare the time. I often said to Jesus, "Let's go farther today than we have ever gone before." Then I set my eyes on Him with absolutely no agenda other than to go deeper into His presence than the previous time. I did this for a period of months with abandon, a practice that today has become a foundation in my life.

Several significant things began to happen to me as I started worshiping consistently and daily. First, I started noticing the healing effect of the daily worship as my body began to respond to the presence of God. I am not passionate about worship because I play, write, and sing worship songs, or because I am a worship leader at a church. I am passionate about worship because without this incredible gift, I doubt that I would be alive today. It has been a healing balm to me physically, emotionally, and spiritually.

I also began to experience an awakening of the prophetic and seeing realm in my life. I found myself suddenly aware of things beyond my ability to perceive naturally. As I worshiped daily, these impressions became stronger, clearer, and more accurate.

The Holy Spirit began to lead me into encounters with the glory of God and heavenly realms. He taught me to wait in His presence until the eyes of my heart became fixed on His glory. He would then take me on journeys and adventures in the spirit world. I have been transported to heaven on numerous occasions and have seen things that are sometimes even too beautiful for words. I will write about some of these experiences in the pages to come. I am a strong believer that an essential element of worship is to be able to "see God."

As I worshiped daily, I began to experience destructive thought patterns and sinful actions dropping off me effortlessly. After a few months of passionate worship, I hardly recognized my own heart. A lifetime of struggles and dark patterns were neutralized in the presence of God. My mind became renewed, addictions were broken, and I became so grateful and in love with Jesus that I hardly knew what to do with myself.

Then another very tender thing began to take place in my heart. Jesus began to strategically arrange a slow but steady return to my calling.

One particular week, the church I attended was missing a bass player for their Sunday morning team, so they asked if I would fill in. At first I protested, but because something in my heart was stirring, I finally agreed to their request.

On that morning, we worshiped through a very simple set of four songs but I was so nervous and emotional, I could hardly even play my instrument. It had been more than a decade since I had been on a church platform, my eyes were brimming with tears, and I could scarcely see my music charts. When it was all over, I quickly made my way off the stage, exited the sanctuary, and hurried down a hallway across from the auditorium.

> *An essential element of worship is to be able to "see God"*

Somehow, I found a janitor's room with an unlocked door and went inside. Sitting there on the floor in the dark, I began to sob my eyes out. In the stillness of that janitor's room, God started to talk with me. He assured me of His love for me and spoke to me about my calling. He told me that if I would surrender to Him, He still had a perfect plan for my life.

I often imagine there were two services happening on that day. First, there was the regular gathering of believers sitting in the sanctuary. Then there was a second, more intimate service going on down the hall in a dark closet filled with Windex and vacuum cleaners. Father God was doing open-heart surgery on one of His broken children, gently hovering His holy presence over him, binding up his wounds, and restoring him to health again. When I finally opened the door to that janitor's room, God had given me a new passion for worship in His house.

A few days later, I went for a walk along a river close to where I lived. I happened upon a place where some rocks jutted out into the current. I used them as stepping-stones to crawl up on a larger rock that was situated right in the middle of the river. I sat there for a period of maybe ten minutes, water flowing around me, when all of a sudden, an audible voice cut through my thoughts: "Dean, would you like to work for a church again?" For a moment I was almost stunned. Then tears came to my eyes as I realized that for years, God had been wooing me back for this very moment. Sitting in the middle of that river, I told my heavenly Father I would love to take Him up on His offer.

> *I have not even scratched the surface of God's goodness in my life*

It was only a couple of months later that an opportunity came to me almost out of nowhere. I ended up, once again, as director of worship at a fairly high-profile church. It was not a position that I should have had by any means. I just happened to be at the right place at the right time and the favor of God was with me. And so, through worship, my life's purpose was restored to me in a short period of time. When worship with no agenda and the presence of God is a priority in our lives, His grace and favor can take you places in weeks that it might take others a lifetime to reach.

As I write today, many other seasons of life and ministry have come and gone. There have been ups and downs, but I continue to worship through them all. I know that I have not even scratched the surface of God's goodness in my life. There will be many more stories in the future as the Holy Spirit reveals the vastness of the thoughts of the Father over me.

In this book, we are going to talk about the story of humankind as it intersects with the gift of worship. We will talk about where it all began, play tag with the storyline as it weaves a thread through the bible, and dream about where it all might end.

The intent of this book is not to present information. There are plenty of resources out there for anyone looking for knowledge on worship. It is important for you to know that I have not come to my conclusions on the subject of worship through studying. Instead, my understanding has come through grace released upon me as I have worshiped. Even at this point in my life, I am encountered time and time again by the glory of heaven. With each encounter, I am left with questions. These questions, along with an unrelenting hunger, draw me forward, and it is from these storehouses that I write.

Chapter 2

NEW BEGINNINGS

Praise the Lord! Praise the Lord from the heavens; praise Him in the heights! Praise Him, all His angels; praise Him, all His hosts! Praise Him sun and moon; praise Him, all stars of light!

(Psalm 148:1-6 ESV)

A few years ago, I had a panoramic vision. Somehow, I was transported to the far reaches of our galaxy. When I looked around, I discovered that I was suspended in outer space and I saw innumerable stars around me. They looked like a virtual pincushion of light against the black space sky. Suddenly I became aware of the most hardcore techno dance track you could ever imagine being blasted out over the vastness of the universe. It was so bass heavy that my entire body shook with every kick drum beat. The galaxy around me began pulsating with the same rhythm, almost in an animated fashion.

I was enjoying the music when I peered into the sky again. To my wonder, all of the stars and constellations were joined together by lines, making stick figures. There were millions of them—as far as the eye could see, and they were dancing as if in a huge, three-dimensional nightclub. What came to my mind immediately was how serious they were about their joy. I began laughing out loud when I saw those stick figure star people. They looked so otherworldly. They were content, happy, delightful, and dancing as if their galaxian lives depended on it.

> *All of creation is filled with the joy of worship from one end to the other*

In a moment my heart came alive with the thought that the entire universe is praising and worshiping at all times. The stars are dancing and all of creation is filled with the joy of worship from one end to the other whether we realize it or not.

Selah – pause in His presence

The book of Genesis has been a personal favorite of mine for years now and it contains many references to worship. The first few mentions are indirect, but as we read on, a clear picture emerges. Eventually we find a worship cornerstone, something we will take the time to put in place before continuing on with our worship journey.

I have always loved the story of the creation of our universe. While others might argue about the validity of various scientific theories, I am brought to tears as I read each and every phrase.

In the beginning, God created ...　　　　　(Genesis 1:1)

If it were up to me to make a list of the most obvious character traits of God, it would probably include such words as merciful, kind, loving, and faithful. However, in the first few words of the bible we find God's premiere character trait. He was creative! In fact, His creativity was so uncontainable that He was compelled to make things—artistic things, things that move and breathe and dance, beautiful things that shine.

In the beginning, God created the heavens ...　　(Genesis 1:1)

The first place that God created was the heavens. Sometime after, God fashioned living beings and angels of all kinds to inhabit His new creative space. Here are some of the most ancient words in the bible found in the book of Job—the oldest book in the bible. These words contain a series of questions that God asked Job:

> *Where were you when I laid the foundations of the earth? Tell me, if you know so much. Who determined its dimensions and stretched out the surveying line? What supports its foundations, and who laid its cornerstone as the morning stars sang together and all the angels shouted for joy?*

(Job 38:4-7)

I have done a fair amount of building in my life. I have determined dimensions on draft boards, stretched out survey lines, and figured out how deep an excavator needs to dig to properly support a footing. I have also been part of crews who have poured foundations of various types.

When the cornerstone of our earth was laid, it was a time of celebration. I am left with a heart full of wonder at the mention of the morning stars singing and the angels shouting for joy. Without doubt, we are witnessing an early account of worship hidden in these verses—one that took place even before our earth was formed.

God's Inaugural Statement

Once the footings of our earth were safely in place, there was still considerable work to be done to make our planet inhabitable. At first, it was formless and void and it was also covered with water. At this stage of creation, I often imagine the earth as a big, round ice cube floating through space. Without light, there is no heat, and the water surrounding our globe would have been frozen solid. Thankfully, God had a plan.

> *Without God's goodness, our entire universe would implode on itself*

> *Then God said, "Let there be light," and there was light. And God saw that the light was good.*

> (Genesis 1:3)

We most often associate light and warmth with our sun, but the sun and the stars were not formed until much later in the process of creation. So, what kind of light did God release in His inaugural statement?

> *God is light, and there is no darkness in him at all.*

> (1 John 1:5)

Every good thing given and every perfect gift is from above, coming down from the Father of lights, with whom there is no variation or shifting shadow.

(James 1:17 NASB)

Our God is the father of all forms of light. God is—light. It is no surprise then, that light is the first thing felt and seen in creation. God used what He had in His hand (light!) to thaw out the earth. Then, for the first four days of creation, He used His glory to illumine the creation process. Glory light is the foundation that our universe rests upon. Even modern-day science tells us that light in the form of photons, is one of the building blocks of matter.

God is Good

God's goodness is another solid layer of bedrock that undergirds creation. God is—good. Without His goodness, our entire universe would implode on itself. Every time God created something new, He saw that it was "good." We are made out of flesh and blood. God is made out of glory light, goodness, and love.

On day three, God created the plants. This is a stumbling block for some people in the timelines of creation since the sun wasn't created until day four. However, if you are of the opinion that God's glory can't grow plants, think again!

Then the angel showed me a river with the water of life, clear as crystal, flowing from the throne of God and of the Lamb. It flowed down the center of the main street. On each side of the river grew a tree of life, bearing twelve crops of fruit, with a fresh crop each month. The leaves were used for medicine to heal the nations. And there will be no night there—no need for lamps or sun—for the Lord God will shine on them.

(Revelation 22:1-2,5)

These verses contain a description of the new heaven and earth. We see rivers, streets, and, yes—plants! We also discover that there is no sunlight, but the Lord himself illuminates the entire scene. God's glory is the purest spectrum of light that exists. I imagine a plant to be very happy in this environment.

The Big Bang!

On the fourth day of creation, God finally created the heavenly bodies.

The sun has one kind of glory, while the moon and stars each have another kind. And even the stars differ from each other in their glory.

(1 Corinthians 15:41)

Creation eventually needed its own reliable source of light, so God lit a large gaseous sphere on fire, transferring the essence of His glory into the sun. The verse above mentions the sun, moon, and stars. I love how it describes their glory. Also notice how each star differs slightly in glory. I recall from my high school science classes that every star has its own unique spectrum of light depending on its chemical makeup.

> *In the garden, I see a most stunning, innocent, and pure picture of worship*

The Crowning Moment of Creation

On day six of the creation process, God formed the land creatures. He then capped off that glorious day by making a supernal class of being, one created in His own image. This new life form had a spirit created to interact with the heavens, a body made to interface with the earth, and also a soul. The soul of the man was given to draw the two worlds together, to give conscious expression, and to make sense out of his existence.

God placed His new creation in the Garden of Eden. We are not told what God talked about with Adam and Eve as they walked together in the cool of the day, but we do know that worship has always been central to our creation. Wherever human civilizations have flourished, worship has always played a major part in one way or another. We also know that after their fall, Adam and Eve hid from the "presence of God." This presence was a constant component of the atmosphere of Eden.

Anyone who has been in a setting where the presence of God is radiant and strong will never dispute this fact: an encounter with God's glory is an invitation to worship. For this reason, the eyes of my heart can't help but imagine Adam and Eve bowing before their God, the Father of creation, and worshiping Him with no restraint. There was no death here, and no pain—just a son and a daughter face to face in intimacy with their Creator. In the garden, even though it is not mentioned directly, I see a most stunning, innocent, and pure picture of worship.

Selah – pause in His presence

Once Adam and Eve fell, God had to make a difficult decision for their own safety. Because He did not want His new creation to go back, eat from the tree of life, and live forever in a fallen state, God had to drive them out of the garden. He then stationed cherubim to guard the pathways back to eternal life. He also made garments of skin for Adam and his wife with which to clothe them.

I would like us to think this situation through for a moment. In the making of this clothing, God had to kill an animal of some kind. Imagine Adam and Eve watching this event. For the first time they witnessed death and blood being shed. Through this event, a stark new reality was unveiled to humankind. Innocent blood was now required to atone for sins. In turn, the skins covered up their shame. Sadly, I see something else hidden in this story. Everything that Adam and Eve knew about worship up until that time had just drastically changed.

These thoughts are mirrored only a few verses later when Cain and Abel, the sons of Adam and Eve, brought offerings to the Lord:

> *At the designated time Cain brought some of the fruit of the ground for an offering to the Lord. But Abel brought some of the firstborn of his flock—even the fattest of them. And the Lord was pleased with Abel and his offering, but with Cain and his offering He was not pleased. So Cain became very angry, and his expression was downcast.*

> (Genesis 4:3-5 NET)

Other translations read, "at the appointed time," or "at the time of harvest." Implied in these verses, is a pre-determined, annual offering of worship and sacrifice. Abel brought the finest firstborn of his flock, complete with the most desirable portions. Cain, on the other hand, brought fruit, something not ordained by the Lord as an acceptable sacrifice. It was for good reason that God had no regard for his offering.

I find it tragic that the first human blood was shed because of jealousy over an offering of worship. My fellow worship leaders should take great comfort in the fact that worship has always been a contentious issue. God eventually told Cain that sin was crouching at the door of his offering. The result of worship not offered in God's per-

> *The first human blood was shed over an offering of worship*

fect order is sin and death. These patterns came into being only a few years into the timelines of life on our planet.

The First Musicians

As we move on just a few verses, we find another inference to music and worship.

> *Adah gave birth to Jabal; he was the father of those who dwell in tents and have livestock. His brother's name was Jubal; he was the father of all those who play the lyre and pipe.*

> (Genesis 4:20-21 NASB)

Here we are told about two brothers. Jabal was a livestock farmer. Then, we meet Jubal, the father of the musicians of our planet. Mentioned here are the lyre—a stringed instrument, and also the pipe—a wind instrument. Right after these verses we meet a third brother, Tubal-cain, who began perfecting the art form of forging bronze and iron. The introduction of music to our planet was simultaneous with the ability to create molten images and idols. Hidden in these words we can find indications of offerings in the livestock, music in the lyres and pipes, and idol worship in the art of forging bronze and iron.

A Soothing Aroma

Only a few chapters later we find the earth destroyed in a catastrophic flood. The world had become corrupted with evil of all kinds. Once again, God had no choice but to take drastic action to protect His creation. Only Noah and his family were saved from annihilation. Immediately following his release from the ark, Noah built an altar and offered burnt sacrifices to the Lord:

> *Noah's offering helped to calm the nerves of our everlasting Father*

Then Noah built an altar to the Lord, and took of every clean animal and of every clean bird and offered burnt offerings on the altar. The Lord smelled the soothing aroma.

(Genesis 8:20-21 NASB)

I can well imagine that God was lost in grief and agitation over that fact that His entire earthbound creation had just been decimated. Because God takes no pleasure in destruction, the millions of souls forever lost in this tragedy would have left Him heart broken. However, Noah's burnt offering was somehow soothing to God. It helped to calm the nerves of our everlasting Father and He, once again, started proclaiming life and blessing over our planet. In these verses, I see the first hints of God making Himself vulnerable to our worship.

Abram's Journey Begins

In Genesis chapter twelve, we are introduced to a new patriarch. Abram was well versed in the art of sacrificing to the Lord. There are numerous mentions of him building altars to the Lord, and God would often speak with him at these times. Along with the details of these offerings, we find the frequent phrase, "And he called upon the name of the Lord." Here is just one example:

> *Then Abram proceeded from there to the mountain on the east of Bethel, and pitched his tent, with Bethel on the west and Ai on the east; and there he built an altar to the Lord and called upon the name of the Lord.*

> (Genesis 12:8 NASB)

The First Worship

If you take a simple bible concordance and look up the word "worship," the very first reference you find will be in the twenty-second chapter of Genesis:

> *Some time later, God tested Abraham's faith. "Abraham!" God called. "Yes," he replied. "Here I am." "Take your only son—yes, Isaac, whom you love so much—and go to the land of Moriah. Go and sacrifice him as a burnt offering on one of the mountains that I will show you."*

> ... *On the third day of their journey, Abraham looked up and saw the place in the distance. "Stay here with the donkey," Abraham told the servants. "The boy and I will travel a little farther. We will **worship** there, and then we will come right back."*

(Genesis 22:1-2,4-5)

In these verses, God asks for a burnt offering and Abraham responds by saying that he and Isaac would go and *worship*. Here we finally have confirmation that previous accounts of burnt offerings mentioned in the bible were, in fact, acts of worship. This passage stands on its own when it comes to the subject of worship. It contains an almost unimaginable story of sacrifice, bringing us much insight as to why we worship, how to worship, and some of the things that happen when we worship. It also unveils one of the redemptive names of God, setting a high standard for worship as it plays out through the rest of the bible.

The story of Abraham and Isaac is the cornerstone of worship that we have been getting ready to lay.

Chapter 3

ABRAHAM AND ISAAC

The Hebrew word translated as "worship" in Abraham's story, is "Shachah." It means to prostrate in homage to royalty, to bow down, or to do reverence. The picture presented in this word speaks of coming before a king or queen, prostrating oneself, and paying homage in the form of a tax or a freewill gift. The idea of bringing something and presenting it as an offering before our God and King is foundational to the definition of worship.

There is also a second Hebrew word that we find periodically translated as "worship." It is "Avodah" and it means jointly—work, worship, and service. This word is most commonly used to describe a life that is constantly laid down before the Lord as a sacrifice of worship. It involves every part of our existence—body, soul, mind, and strength.

With, "Shachah," the worship is more of an event that is celebrated either individually or corporately. With "Avodah," we find a seamless 24/7 lifestyle of worship. These two

Hebrew words combine to create an understanding of worship in a similar way to a two-sided coin.

With these definitions in place, I believe there are times in all of our lives where God tests our resolve to worship Him in a way that is far outside of our comfort zone. In the moment, the circumstances often seem extreme and bizarre, but I have learned that God always knows what He is doing—He always has our best interests in mind.

A Big Stretch

My wife and I got a very late start on some of the things that many other couples wisely put in place early in their relationship. We spent so much of our lives travelling the world and playing music, that years went by before we even thought of settling down long enough to do something basic, like buy a house. Once we started considering where we were in life, we had very little in the way of possessions—certainly nothing even close to what was needed for a down payment.

My work at the time was very unstable. I was working on a contract basis and would get paid every few months when the jobs were finished. This created a feast or famine situation in our lives. Even so, the desire to buy a house just wouldn't go away. It only seemed to grow stronger with each passing month. We would print out piles of real estate listings in our area and go for drives, dreaming of the day when we would be homeowners.

Eventually, we found our dream house. It was on a small acreage and it was priced ridiculously above our qualification level—which was next to nothing. At the time, it was vacant, so one night we drove out to the property and parked in front of the driveway. We held hands and asked our heavenly Father if He would give it to us.

The next day, I went out for a walk. I was happily strolling along, dreaming about our house plans, when I heard the voice of the Holy Spirit clearly ask me to give away a large sum of money to a ministry that I knew was struggling. As it turned out, I had just wrapped up two major contracts and gotten paid, but the number I heard was all of what I had just made and more.

> *At times, God tests our resolve to worship Him in a way that is far outside our comfort zone*

It was an amount so uncomfortable for me that it might as well have been all the money in the world. I sat down on a log and began to tremble as my mind tried to reason through the ramifications of what I had just heard.

After returning from my walk, I conferred with my wife and then wrote out the check. My hands were cold and clammy and my stomach was unsettled. The next morning, after a sleepless night, I contacted the ministry, and dropped off the check. I felt absolutely numb all day long, wondering how we were going to pay our rent and buy food for the foreseeable future.

I went to bed that night still in a state of shock, and was staring bleakly at the ceiling when I had an open vision. I saw a pile of split logs that were arranged in a teepee fashion over an offering of some kind. Then a bolt of fire appeared from above the logs and consumed the wood and the offering under it all in one grand puff. It almost looked humorous—like an animated gif.

The next day, I went for another walk and Jesus started talking to me in a way that I had never heard Him before. His voice was clear and unmistakable. He gave me specific words, spoke direction into my life, and stabilized the course that my life was on.

Within a week, I had a permanent job offered to me from a place that I was not expecting. I no longer had to do contract work, my income source was stable, and I was earning significantly more than I had been before. I was at that job for several years and enjoyed every minute of it.

Within a couple of months, two large lump sums of money came to us from the most unexpected of sources. Together the amounts added up to an almost twenty percent down payment. We soon put in an offer on the same house that we had asked God for and we became homeowners— not of just any house, but of our dream acreage.

The breakthroughs that we experienced in relation to our first home came about because I somehow found the courage to follow God's voice and offer up a sacrifice of worship that was far above my ability to comprehend.

In the months that followed, I was led to the story of Abraham and Isaac. Since that time, I have found myself wrapped up in the different phrases of Genesis chapter twenty-two more times than I can remember.

Selah – pause in His presence

When I read the account of Abraham's sacrifice, my heart is touched to the core. What strikes me is that this incident marks the apparent end of a dream, one authored by God Himself.

God came to Abraham when he was in his mid-seventies, graced him with the promise of a son, and then confirmed it with a blood covenant. God also gave Abraham a powerful visual of his descendants being as numerous as the stars in the heavens.

I am not sure how long you might have believed God for something—a promise, a healing, the salvation of a loved one, or the fulfillment of destiny in some way or another. Personally, I have believed for certain things for many years. I am overwhelmed when I think of how Abraham believed for nearly a quarter of a century for Isaac.

As with all faith journeys, there would have been ups and downs, good and bad days, nights when all the stars in the sky were vibrant and viewable, and others when the sky was blanketed in cloud cover. When Isaac was finally born, there was great joy in the house of Abraham and Sarah. Isaac's name means "laughter."

Think of Isaac growing into a young man of almost fifteen years of age. If you add this number together with the twenty-five years that Abraham and Sarah believed for Isaac, you have almost forty years! Now listen to these words:

> *Take your only son—yes, Isaac, whom you love so much—and go to the land of Moriah. Go and **sacrifice** him as a burnt offering on one of the mountains that I will show you.*

> (Genesis 22:1-2)

Always a Sacrifice

Sacrifice – *The act of offering something precious to a deity, to surrender up something that is costly for the sake of something even more valuable, to dispose of goods regardless of profit for a higher cause*

As I ponder Abraham's story, one thing invariably captures me—worship is always a sacrifice. That which we lay down, no matter how costly, is destined for the fire, never to be seen again.

In Abraham's case, he had a thorough understanding of sacrifices and burnt offerings. He knew that in the end, only a pile of smoldering ashes would remain on that altar. By all indications, this sacrifice of worship would terminate a forty-year dream. It was an offering to which no earthly value could ever compare.

In my own journey, I have learned that if worshiping God doesn't cost me something, it is not worship at all. There have been times when I have tried to worship without sacrifice, but it always leaves me empty and agitated. If I bring nothing to the altar, there is no sacrifice, no fire,

> *I have learned that if worshiping doesn't cost me something, it is not worship at all*

and no life to be found. In the end, it only amounts to a form of religion instead of true worship.

Obedience is Key

I have also discovered that obedience is an integral part of worship. There are always numerous chances to take, promptings to consider, and unknown roads to travel when following the leading of the Holy Spirit in worship. However, these next few phrases take obeying the voice of God to a whole new level.

> *The next morning Abraham got up early. He saddled his donkey and took two of his servants with him, along with his son, Isaac. Then he chopped wood for a fire for a burnt offering and set out for the place God had told him about.*

(Genesis 22:3)

My respect for Abraham is heightened when I think of how he got up extra early that morning. I can only imagine the sleepless night he must have had as he considered what he was about to do. His mental and emotional faculties would have, no doubt, been in a state of shock. Yet he got his axe, split a pile of wood, and started on his journey with a stunning display of prompt obedience.

Lift Up Your Eyes

In this next verse, I find another side of the worship cornerstone—it opens up the "seeing" realm.

> *On the third day Abraham raised his eyes and saw the place from a distance.*

(Genesis 22:4 NASB)

Worship always involves lifting the eyes of our heart toward heaven—it awakens us to see. I used to be a person who would listen to stories of people with visions, dreams, and spiritual seeing adventures with great suspicion. However, when I started making daily worship a priority, my inner eyes became acclimated to a whole new world. There have been numerous encounters along my journey, and I now anticipate my eyes being opened in some unique way each time I worship.

All by Faith

Another thing I have noticed with Abraham is the amount of faith with which he spoke—not just once, but several times.

> *"Stay here with the donkey," Abraham told the servants. "The boy and I will travel a little farther. We will worship there, and then we will come right back." As the two of them walked on together, Isaac turned to Abraham and said, "Father?" "Yes, my son?" Abraham replied. "We have the fire and the wood," the boy said, "but where is the sheep for the burnt offering?" "God will provide a sheep for the burnt offering, my son," Abraham answered.*

(Genesis 22:5,7-8)

I have often wondered what emotional strength, if any, Abraham had left at this point in his journey. Even so, every word he spoke, he said with faith. In his mind, two of them were going to worship, and somehow two of them would also be returning. When Isaac questioned him about the sheep, Abraham again responded with faith, declaring that God would provide.

With a precedent setting event like this, you would expect there to be a large crowd in the bleachers

The book of Hebrews contains another passage that gives a window into the thoughts of Abraham as he and Isaac walked toward the sacrifice that day:

> *It was by faith that Abraham offered Isaac as a sacrifice when God was testing him. Abraham reasoned that if Isaac died, God was able to bring him back to life again. And in a sense, Abraham did receive his son back from the dead.*

(Hebrews 11:17,19)

Here we discover that Abraham believed that God would raise Isaac up from the dead, right out of those smoldering ashes if necessary. Worship always requires faith. Once we place something on the altar, we entrust it to God with an open hand knowing that somehow, He will give back to us more than we ever give up.

The Point of No Return

Every time I read the next few verses in Abraham's story, my heart has a different emotional response. Sometimes I feel pain, sometimes I am filled with joy, other times I gravitate toward awe or wonder. Making a sacrifice of worship often encompasses the far ends of the emotional spectrum.

I also find these phrases release a strong sense of the presence of God over me. In them, I see extreme and authentic worship. There was no agenda to be found in what Abraham was about to do. He had no idea what the outcome might be. His only motivations were love, devotion, and the reverential fear of God. With a precedent setting event like this you would expect there to be a large crowd in the bleachers, but the only person watching was the worthy one—the Lord God. This was truly an audience of one.

> *When they arrived at the place where God had told them to go, Abraham built an altar and arranged the wood on it. Then he tied his son, Isaac, and laid him on the altar on top of the wood. And Abraham picked up the knife to kill his son as a sacrifice.*

(Genesis 22:9-10)

Selah – pause in His presence

I don't think there is any question that Abraham had started the downward stroke of his knife before the Lord called out to him that day. There is no other way to worship but with all we have and all we are—to the point of no return.

Over the years, these verses have given rise to some questions that are never far from my mind when I worship. When I come before God, what am I bringing as a sacrifice? Is it something that is costly to me? Is it precious? Is it something I love? Is it my very best offering? What does binding and laying something on the altar mean for me in this moment? If I had a knife right now, what would it look like? Am I surrendering all?

The Voice of God

> *At that moment the angel of the Lord called to him from heaven, "Abraham! Abraham!" "Yes," Abraham replied, "Here I am!" "Don't lay a hand on the boy!" the angel said. "Do not hurt him in any way, for now I know that you truly fear God. You have not withheld from me your son, your only son."*

(Genesis 22:11-12)

I used to wonder why God would talk to me so clearly after I had worshiped. Some of my most life altering words from heaven have come in the aftermath of my most costly offerings. Often, the time leading up to a sacrifice will be filled with uncomfortable silence and questions

> *There is no other way to worship but with all we have and all we are*

for me. By contrast, the moments after will be a waterfall of prophetic downloads, clear direction from the Holy Spirit, and revelation.

In the events after the first official sacrifice of worship in the bible, Abraham was caught up in a prophetic slipstream so significant that it altered both his future and also the course of history from that point on.

Eyes Lifted X 2

*Then Abraham **lifted his eyes** and looked, and there behind him was a ram caught in the thicket by its horns. So Abraham went and took the ram, and offered it up for a burnt offering instead of his son.*

(Genesis 22:13 NKJV)

These verses mention the seeing realm for a second time. In the moments directly following worship, I have learned to wait, listen, and lift my eyes to see what heaven is doing.

Yahweh-Yireh

There are several places in the bible where God allows Himself to be known in a specific way. On these occasions, a name is assigned to God in a hyphenated form. The first part of the name is always "Jehovah," and the second part is a character trait—a side of God that is being highlighted at the time.

The first place where God is revealed in this manner is right after Abraham's sacrifice of worship. It is here that God becomes known as Jehovah-Jireh (Yahweh-Yireh).

> *Abraham named the place Yahweh-Yireh (which means "the Lord will provide"). To this day, people still use that name as a proverb: "On the mountain of the Lord it will be provided."*

(Genesis 22:14)

That day, up on Mount Moriah, God eternal didn't just walk up and introduce Himself to Abraham as Jehovah-Jireh. Instead, Abraham had a personal revelation of God as he worshiped. He named the place of worship after his encounter and from that moment on, left a legacy for anyone who would follow.

I have climbed many mountains of uncertainty in my life. There have been many times where I have felt the calling of the Holy Spirit to offer up unusual sacrifices—things I did not understand. He has asked me to give extraordinary monetary gifts, to lay down communities that I have loved, to sell houses, and to move away from friends. A few years ago, Jesus asked me to give up a job that I enjoyed immensely. He has also asked me to surrender dreams that I have held dear, things that have represented years of investment, prayer, and faith for me.

> *In every act of surrender, you have just exercised extreme wisdom; you have worshiped*

Every time I come to one of these altars, I am left with only one thing to hold on to—the example of Abraham. He was the first person to climb this mountain and I am eternally grateful that he left a flagpole at the top with a standard that reads, *"The Lord Will Provide."* When I see that banner, still flying strong after all these years, it gives me courage to lift up my eyes and make my own sacrifice. I have learned the Faithful One will never be out given.

For a moment, I would like to encourage those of you who are climbing your own mountain of worship. Every time you lay down your will on the altar, every time you offer up praise when nothing is going right, whenever you lift your eyes in the middle of turmoil and bring a sacrifice of color and joy, through every song you sing, every time you dance, and in every act of surrender—you have just exercised extreme wisdom. You have worshiped!

You have also set yourself up for Jehovah-Jireh to come by your side and provide the answer you do not see right now. Keep lifting your eyes. God is with you and His angels have been dispatched on your behalf. He knows all, He has received your sacrifice, and He will not forget! These are the promises of worship offered in faith and obedience!

Words of Hope

In earlier chapters, I mentioned that the calling on my life was unlocked in the span of a few short months as I worshiped without restraint. With Abraham, a similar thing happened. He received a word of hope so far reaching that it affected the way heaven viewed earth. For all eternity, we will live under the blessing of the statement, "We are the seed of Abraham."

> *Then the angel of the Lord called again to Abraham from heaven. "This is what the Lord says: Because you have obeyed me and have not withheld even your son, your only son, I swear by my own name that I will certainly bless you. I will multiply your descendants beyond number, like the stars in the sky and the sand on the seashore. And through your descendants all the nations of the earth will be blessed—all because you have obeyed me."*

(Genesis 22:15-18)

I would like to finish laying our cornerstone of worship by saying that the first account of worship in the bible opened the door for our redemption. Some might think that God does not need such an opening, that He can intervene in our world anytime He likes. This is only partially true.

Imagine for a moment that you have a house and you lease it out to someone for a year. Even though you are the legal owner of the house, during the lease period, you will have limited access to your property.

Our earth is much the same. After creating our world, God gave it to humankind. We, in turn, relinquished it to the devil.

> *Then the devil led him* [Jesus] *up to a high place and showed him in a flash all the kingdoms of the world. And he said to him, "To you I will grant this whole realm—and the glory that goes along with it, for it has been relinquished to me, and I can give*

it to anyone I wish. So then, if you will worship me, all this will be yours." Jesus answered him, "It is written, 'You are to worship the Lord your God and serve only him.'"

(Luke 4:5-8 NET)

The devil is an extreme legalist. Had God intervened in our world by any means other than a perfect plan, the devil would have forever contested Jesus' entering of our world and His victory on the cross. Because Abraham obeyed God, freely offering his only son in worship, it created a window for God to reach down into our world and give us His only Son. In the ultimate act of worship on the cross, Jesus made a way for us to return to the garden again.

> *The first account of worship in the bible opened the door for our redemption*

Knowing what was at stake that day on Mount Moriah only heightens my sense of awe over this stunning display of surrender and worship.

Someday, I will be highly honored to meet Abraham. His fatherly anointing was so significant that he became known as the father of faith, the father of many nations, and the father of those who inherit the promises of God. But in my estimation, one of Abraham's most understated characteristics is that he is the father of worship.

Selah – pause in His presence

Chapter 4

MOSES AND THE GLORY

The book of Genesis has many other accounts of sacrificial worship interlaced with the stories of our early fathers of faith. Isaac was a dedicated worshiper, as well as Jacob, Levi, and Joseph.

If sacrifice is the cornerstone of worship, then the walls of the house are built out of God's glory. When we turn the pages of our bible over to Exodus, worship takes on a new dimension—it becomes all about the glory of God.

Physics Anyone?

God's glory was part of creation right from the beginning. At first, it existed in the spirit realm, but when God said, *"Let there be light,"* He also disbursed it into the natural realm. For this reason, glory crosses over. It can co-exist both in heaven and on earth at the same time. It is the ultimate kingdom building matter. From the start, it has been the plan of God for the earth to be filled with His glory.

There is something in the world of physics known as the "Law of the Conservation of Energy." This law states that energy can neither be created nor destroyed in a closed system, only converted from one form to another. In simple terms, our universe is a closed system. It exists with a fixed amount of stored up energy. That energy can take on different shapes, but it can never be added to or taken away from.

God's glory is similar—it exists in a closed system. The source of all glory is God. Since it proceeds from Him, it all needs to be returned back to Him. Statements such as, "All glory belongs to God," or "He is the only one worthy of glory," are not just semantics. They are literal. Glory is never ours. It is on loan from the Father of lights and He graciously shines it on all that He has made.

Everything created has been painted with a brush stroke of glory—every life form, every person, and every heavenly body like the sun, moon, and stars. Worship is the channel through which this glory is brought back to its source. For this reason, all of creation constantly engages in worship.

So exactly what is the presence of God, or in other words, His glory? It is a substance that materializes from the radiance of the face of God. Because it is so saturated with life, it has infinite creative and restorative powers—our entire universe was fashioned in its cradle. It drips with love, nourishes, and sustains all things. It manifests as light, smoke, a cloud, a glowing mass of incandescent ambience, an all-consuming fire, lightning-like flashes, or a weighty presence in a room. It is both illumination and atmosphere proceeding from the countenance of the Almighty. Without it, everything we know would cease to exist, and without it, worship is meaningless.

The Boat Show

My wife and I have a love for anything that has to do with the ocean. A few years ago, we went to the international boat show, held annually in the city where we live. It was an unusual day for me. As we walked up and down the rows of boats and yachts, I kept noticing that the presence of God was resting strongly on me. It was so intense that I was constantly distracted. I had to sit down in the stands a few times and breathe before carrying on.

> *Everything created has been painted with a brush stroke of glory*

After we got home, I went into my study and prayed in the spirit for two full hours. The glory of God seemed to wash over me like a waterfall until I was thoroughly undone. I kept asking Jesus what He was doing, but I heard nothing. My questions were only met with more glory. Finally I went to bed, and that night I had an encounter that forever changed me.

I dreamed that I was driving up a hill. It was lush and green and there were sheep grazing on the slopes. The road eventually ended so I got out of the car and continued on foot up the pathway. As I rounded the crest of the hill, I realized this was no ordinary landscape—it was actually heaven.

When I looked down, I saw the path I was walking on was made out of golden paving stones. They were about two feet square and their surfaces were brushed in opposite directions to each other, giving the look of a checkerboard. A short distance later, the path gave way to a round feature area. I have created many floor mosaics in my days of building and tile laying, but the golden pavers in this area were arranged in such exquisite patterns that I was left in a state of wonder. The center tile was so beautiful I began crying.

I finally gathered up enough strength to shift my gaze from the pathway and look up at what was around me. Situated on the edge of the hill were five large mansions. They were on plots of land that were two or three acres each. They all had stunning panoramic views of the surrounding countryside and they had aqua blue lakes in their back yards. In the distance were rivers, valleys, trees, and mountains.

My eyes were drawn back to the center golden tile so I went over and kneeled down in the middle of it. I put my hands out, closed my eyes, and said, "This is where I wait until the glory comes."

No sooner had I spoken, than I heard a rushing sound and the glory of heaven completely engulfed me. I collapsed on the golden pavement, too overcome to even move as the glory pulsed around me for what seemed like a minute or two. Eventually, the force of the light lifted me up off the ground and into the sky. From my new, elevated viewpoint, I could see the expanses of paradise and a great shining city off in the distance. Then I felt someone grasp me under my arms from behind. I knew it was Holy Spirit.

> *God truly loves to reveal His glory to those who will be bold enough to ask*

Holy Spirit started twirling me around in circles like a parent would play with a child. I started laughing and worshiping all at the same time—there was nothing else I could do. Wave upon wave of glory crashed over me as I worshiped and praised in circle after circle. When the turning finally stopped and my arms were released, I began to slowly drift back to the ground until I was left kneeling on that same beautiful tile—overwhelmed beyond comprehension. I was a mess of tears, reverence, and silence. As I woke up, I was so overcome with glory that I hardly knew where I was. The presence of God lingered on me for almost two days.

As I began to unpack what had happened, I realized that a constant cry of my heart for months had been for God to show me His glory. I would get up in the morning praying for the glory, go to bed crying out for the glory, and with every moment in between, I would ask to see God's glory. To this day, I am still humbled at how God answered me. In the years following this encounter, I have not stopped asking God to show me His glory. I have discovered that God truly loves to reveal His glory to those who will be bold enough to ask.

Selah – pause in His presence

Let it Burn

While Abraham had an understanding of sacrificial worship, Moses had another bent. He had a soft spot for the glory.

Moses' first encounter with God's glory was in the wilderness while tending sheep. He noticed a bush that was burning but not being consumed by the fire. At first he was afraid of it, but once God started speaking, Moses took off his shoes and put down his staff. In the glory of God, all earthly plans are surrendered. God is the only one who holds an agenda when His glory is on display. After this experience, Moses was undoubtedly wrecked.

God's glory was Moses' constant companion from that time forward. It was with him as he went back to deliver God's chosen people from slavery. It was also present in the pillar of fire and the cloud that led the Israelites through the wilderness. It provided food and water, protection, and shelter. Every time a miracle would happen, credit would be given to the matchless glory of God.

Eventually, the Israeli camp came to Mount Sinai, the same place where Moses had originally seen the burning bush. God's glory descended on the mountain in the form of smoke, lightning, and fire. God then called Moses up onto the mountain and gave him a message for His people:

> *Now if you will obey me and keep my covenant, you will be my own special treasure from among all the peoples on earth; for all the earth belongs to me. And you will be my kingdom of priests, my holy nation.*

> (Exodus 19:5)

It seems to me that the Levitical system of worship, established a short while later, was not God's original plan. God's heart was to make every individual in that vast camp, one of His priests. He wanted an entire kingdom of face-to-face worshipers—every person having access to a personal relationship with His glory and holiness.

However, when the Israelites witnessed the glory of God firsthand, they feared for their lives. They viewed Him as angry and threatening rather than loving and nurturing. With little understanding of the true nature of the God who was wooing them, they rejected His offer—opting for Moses

> *In the glory of God, all earthly plans are surrendered*

as spokesperson between them and God. This decision eventually led to the establishment of Aaron and the single tribe of Levi as the priestly core.

I often wonder if God's heart was broken by this decision. Even thousands of years later, His desire is still the same.

> *All glory to him who loves us and has freed us from our sins by shedding his blood for us. He has made us a Kingdom of priests for God his Father.*

> (Revelation 1:5-6)

The Lord then called Moses back to the mountain. The very glory of God that had frightened the children of Israel was still present, but by this time, Moses had already encountered God's glory numerous times. Even though the cloud looked luminous, he was confident in what was behind the glory—God's unconditional love. Instead of being afraid, Moses deliberately entered the cloud.

There, in the middle of the fire and the smoke, God issued the Ten Commandments to Moses. The very first statute was the law of worship. There were to be no graven images and the people were to worship the Lord God alone.

However, when Moses took longer than expected on the mountain, the camp below became restless. Their sense of identity at this point in their journey was paper-thin—they wanted to know God but they had very little history with Him and they felt vulnerable.

The need to worship is such a basic human instinct. Worshiping God, the Father of all creation, grounds us and sets a solid foundation for our lives and future. Moses' prolonged absence exposed a void in God's people, one of fear and insecurity. Out of this vacuum, the Israelites began exploring other options for worship.

Worship Gone Wrong

*God spoke to Moses, "Go! Get down there! Your people whom you brought up from the land of Egypt have fallen to pieces. In no time at all they've turned away from the way I commanded them: They made a molten calf and **worshiped** it. They've **sacrificed** to it and said, 'These are the gods, O Israel, that brought you up from the land of Egypt!'"*

(Exodus 32:7-8 MSG)

As Moses hurried back toward the camp along with his mentee, Joshua, they heard *"the sound of **singing**"* in the valley. (Exodus 32:18)

Worship, singing, and sacrifice—these three words combine to describe the first account of idolatry in the bible, and it is sadly attributed to God's own people. After this point, countless other horrific stories of idol worship appear throughout the Old Testament. Somehow, turning away from God in order to serve things created by our own hands is a tragic tendency for humans.

Idol worship can be deliberate and blatant, but it can also be very subtle. There have been many occasions where I have come face to face with idols even in my own life. We readily slip into idolatry when we act out of fear, choosing to live outside of God's timing. We

> *Turning away from God to serve things created by our own hands is a tragic tendency for humans*

start designing alternative plans for our lives. Sometimes we also take good things given to us by God and elevate them to a wrongful place in our lives, making idols out of them.

To feed the monster we have created, we sacrifice to it in order to keep it alive. The offerings are made by diverting resources to maintain it, or by using up precious human life force to sustain it. Whenever I find myself in a position of burnout or perpetual lack, I start to look for idols—they are sure to be right around the corner. There is no Jehovah-Jireh in idol worship. In simple terms, it is called "doing things in our own strength."

Show Me Your Glory

A short while later, the Lord called Moses up on the mountain again. God was intent on abandoning the Israelites, but Moses began interceding for them. He told God that if His presence did not go with them, they were not going anywhere. Eventually Moses cried out boldly to God, *"Show me your glorious presence!"* God responded with these words:

The LORD replied, "I will make all my goodness pass before you, and I will call out my name, Yahweh, before you. But you may not look directly at my face, for no one may see me and live." The LORD continued, "Look, stand near me on this rock. As my glorious presence passes by, I will hide you in the crevice of the rock and cover you with my hand until I have passed by. Then I will remove my hand and let you see me from behind."

(Exodus 33:19-22)

There are four pillars of our house of worship found in these verses—the presence of God, the glory of God, the goodness of God, and the light of the countenance of the face of God. These four corner columns are so closely intertwined that, at times, they are indistinguishable from each other.

God's presence is the manifestation of His glory here on this earth. In my experience, the presence of God has an atmospheric and heartwarming characteristic, whereas the glory will bring physical characteristics like heat, light, clouds, and luminance. Moses asked to see a combo of God's "glorious presence." Glory and presence are as inseparable as sun and light.

> *A request to see God's glory is a request to see God's face*

God responded to Moses' request by saying that He would pass all of His goodness before him. It is no accident that when God created light, it was punctuated by the phrase,

"And God saw that it was good." God's glory and His goodness are one and the same.

God told Moses that He could not see His face and live. Here we find another aspect of the glory—the countenance of God. Moses had little idea of what he was asking for that day. He didn't know a request to see God's glory was a request to see God's face, the source of the glory. For this rea- ...Moses with His hand so he wouldn't ...posure on that rocky ledge.

...ge contains a word with two inter- ...is the word "paneh." Translated di- ...," and also "face." To seek God's ...ek to be in a position where God's ...onversely, to seek God's face, is to ...God's glory is the radiance of the ...e.

...ing Low

...Lord passed in front of Moses, ...s out as one of my favorites in the ...ncountered by glory every time I read it.

> *And Moses quickly bowed his head toward the earth and worshiped.*

(Exodus 34:8 ESV)

To be in the glorious presence of God is to understand one thing—the glory, the presence, God's goodness, and the light of God's countenance is the only thing needed to inspire

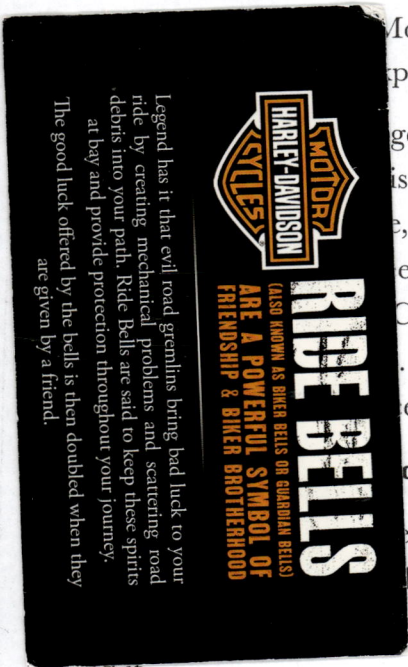

worship. God's glory is the singular star of the show. It is the essential element, the "one thing," and the pearl of great price. It evokes a natural response in us, bringing us to our knees.

Someday, every created thing in the universe will bow in worship at the revealing of God's glory—and every tongue will have no choice but to confess that Jesus is Lord *"To the glory of God the Father!"*

Veil Please!

Once back at the Israeli camp, Moses' face was shining so brightly from His brush with God's glory, that He had to cover it with a veil. Just a few years ago, I witnessed something similar. I was at a conference where the presence of God rested strongly for three days. On the final night, when the speaker got up, I noticed that his face had a slight but definite glow to it.

In Moses' case, he would often go into the tent of meeting where he would commune with God. Once behind the curtain, he would remove the veil and his face would be recharged with radiant glory. In these actions, Moses left a stunning heritage for us when it comes to meeting face-to-face with God.

> *So all of us who have had that veil removed can see and reflect the glory of the Lord. And the Lord—who is the Spirit—makes us more and more like Him as we are changed into his glorious image.*

(2 Corinthians 3:18)

My heart burns when I read these words. There is little else that matters to me except to be in a place where the face of God is turned toward me and His glory shines on me. I find that here I am transformed effortlessly. Worship has always been about the effect of God's glory on our hearts. We bring our lives and lay them down at His feet. In turn, He graces us with His presence and we are changed into His image.

Selah – pause in His presence

A Very Fancy Tent!

Moses then started on a very aggressive building project—the construction of the wilderness tabernacle. When finished, it bore a stunning prophetic representation to God's redemptive plan, and it became the central gathering place for worship. The ark of the covenant, sitting inside the holy of holies, became the resting place for God's presence. Worship in the shadow of the tabernacle took on a definitive purpose. It became about God's glory.

Worship has always been about the effect of God's glory on our hearts

The tabernacle fire was ignited by God's glory and it was kept burning 24/7. Against this backdrop, God's people brought their sacrifices. At times, the glory of God would fall from heaven and consume what was on the altar. At other times, the offerings would simply be burnt in the presence of the Lord.

Certain portions of the offerings were used to supply the Levites and their families with food as they served God's people around the tabernacle. Other offerings were waved before the Lord. God's glory often filled the entire tabernacle and the tent of meeting. Blood from the most crucial sacrifices was brought right into the most holy place and sprinkled on the mercy seat and the ark.

There was no singing, no sound systems, no light shows, no worship leaders, and no Christian worship radio stations at this time. There were no worship seminars and no multimillion selling worship albums. Worship simply and beautifully embodied the word "Shachah"—to prostrate in homage to royalty, to bow, and to do reverence. God's people would come and bring their sacrifices (that which was due Him) to the tabernacle, and humbly offer them in the presence of His glory.

Everything within me longs for a return to these simple patterns today. In the wilderness tabernacle, I see a beautiful picture of God's people gathering together for one purpose—to meet with Him. I also see worship and the glory of God as the first priority. Without God's glory, sacrifices or worship, as honest and sincere as they might be, remain unburned.

There is only one legitimate consumer of worship—the consuming glory fire of God. There is also only one Being qualified to receive worship—the God to whom all glory is due.

Chapter 5

THE LEVITES

*About this time, a man and a woman from the **tribe of Levi** got married. The woman became pregnant and gave birth to a son. She saw that he was a special baby and kept him hidden for three months.*

(Exodus 2:1-2)

The verses we have just read describe the birth and lineage of Moses, the man who loved God's glory. By the end of Moses' life, there was such a significant development of friendship between him and God that he was eulogized as a prophet of unmatched distinction—one whom "God knew face to face."

Not many realize that Moses was the youngest of three siblings—all of them full blood members of the tribe of Levi. Together, this family had a profound impact on the global worshiping community, not only in their generation, but also for thousands of years to come. Moses' sister was named Miriam and he had a brother named Aaron.

Miriam was a prophetess, dancer, musician, and singer. She wrote one of the most recognizable songs of the Old Testament after the Egyptian army was thrown into the Red Sea. She was extremely influential as a leader, especially when the children of Israel were making their way through the wilderness.

Aaron was a natural born leader and a prophet. He was an unusually gifted public speaker and he became Moses' spokesperson, declaring the word of the Lord to those in his path. He had a significant gift of miracles working through him. Power and authority resonated in both his words and actions. The anointing of worship was so strong on Aaron, that God chose him to be the father of the entire Levitical priesthood.

While the book of Exodus is about Moses, the journey of the Israelites, and the glory of God, the book of Leviticus is dedicated to the priesthood instituted by Aaron. If the walls of our worship house are built out of glory, then the Levites are the workers who caretake the worship of the house of the Lord.

Getting Personal

Ever since I can remember, I have had a song in my heart. It is like a playlist without end. Sometimes it is loud, drowning out all my thoughts to the point of distraction. Other times I think it is gone, but if I am still for a moment, I hear it—persistently taking up space in the depths of my soul. Even at night, the song relentlessly serenades me.

As a small child, I found that I had a keen, inbuilt fascination for anything to do with music, instruments, recording machines, and church. From an early age, hardly a week has gone by where I haven't been involved in serving the worship of God's people in some way. I have been on many stages, played instruments, sang, gone on missions trips, and toured all over the world. I have also led numerous services, small groups, retreats, and workshops. Music and worship have been my life. When I am engaged in facilitating the worship of God's house, I often have the sense that this is what I was born to do.

> *The anointing of worship was so strong on Aaron, that God chose him to be the father of the entire Levitical priesthood*

I have been privileged to work alongside many gifted worshipers in my lifetime. There have been singers, instrumentalists, dancers, artists, writers, recording artists, graphic artists, and dramatic actors. There have also been makeup artists, photographers, costume makers, stage directors, sound and lighting technicians, and choreographers.

Along with these people, my life has crossed paths with numerous church leaders who could do many things with their lives, but they choose to serve week after week—loving the people of God, calling them up, speaking God's word over them, and walking alongside them in many diverse situations. The people I have described have some of the most unselfish, humble, and beautiful hearts on the face of our planet.

I have often wondered what makes these individuals who they are—why the gifts and callings of their lives are so unshakable. I have also pondered why I couldn't break free from what is so entrenched in my own heart. There have been several times I have tried to escape my destiny, but each time I would try to go a different direction in life, I would end up despondent and downcast.

Finally, one day I was having coffee with a mentor and friend. We were discussing these thoughts when he looked at me and said, "Dean, the reason is simple—you are a Levite." In that moment, it was like a light bulb went on inside my heart. For the first time in my life, I understood who I was. I was finally able to stop fighting against myself, accept how God had made me, and embrace who I was born to be.

The fact is, I am a marked person—one born to serve in the house of the Lord. My spiritual lineage comes from the family of Moses, Miriam, and Aaron. I was set apart from birth like Samuel, and given as a gift to God's people. I have been called into the tent of meeting, up onto the mountain of God's glory, and into the holy place. I am a person who has been brought face to face with God and at times I have been given words for His people. I was born to lead God's people into worship and into His presence.

> *The priests wore something called an ephod—a device that could tell if a matter was true or not*

Selah – pause in His presence

The Set Apart Ones

The Levites made up one entire tribe of the children of Israel. Their official status as "set apart ones" began in the wilderness. Aaron was appointed as Israel's first priest, and from that point in time, his family was selected by God to care for the wilderness tabernacle and everything pertaining to the worship of God's people.

The first Levites had an inspiring set of responsibilities. They kept the tabernacle in good repair, baked the bread of the presence, and made oils and ointments. They also offered up sacrifices—including animal sacrifices of various kinds, grain offerings, wave offerings, and offerings of incense.

The priests, in particular, were responsible to hear the word of the Lord for the people in many different situations. They wore something called an ephod—a device that could tell if a matter was true or not. Often, the leaders and kings of Israel would seek them out to bring God's counsel in confusing times, or to help when difficult decisions needed to be made.

In the wilderness, every time the glory cloud of God began to move, the Levites completely dismantled the tabernacle, carried it to the next location, and reassembled it again. The most crucial part of this operation was the transportation of the ark of the covenant. Two long poles were inserted through a set of rings, one on each side of the ark. Then, four designated priests carried the ark on foot, the ends of the poles resting on their shoulders.

Eventually, the Israelites settled into their promised land. The Levites continued to administer the order of worship for God's people, but now from an established location. They offered up sacrifices, received tithes, and brought leadership and counsel where needed. As the people of Israel spread out over their new homeland and built cities, Levites were stationed in each district to carry out the duties of worship for the citizens.

Under the rule of king David, the role of the Levites was elevated to a whole new level. Their status became one of great honor as they served day and night in the house of the Lord. They played instruments, sang, worshiped, led processions, kept city gates, upkept books and records, and maintained all aspects of the worship of God's people. As a Levite, this era was the greatest Old Testament time frame to be alive.

Fun Facts

Here are a few facts about the Levites. They were born into their calling, chosen and set apart by God. A young Levite's training was specifically tailored to his or her future as a servant of worship and of the house of the Lord.

The Levites were not given an inheritance of land with the rest of the Israelites. It was said that "God, Himself," was their heritage. For this reason, they were considered civil servants of their country and were exempt from military service. They were paid full time, competitive wages through the tabernacle treasury, and all of their living expenses were also covered. They were given places to live, sometimes on the walls of the cities—places with a view. My heart is touched when I think of how the Lord God knew His set apart ones would need inspiration. For this reason, He

> *If you are a Levite, there is little you can do to escape your destiny*

supplied them with everything needed for a peaceful, stress free environment in which to live, serve, and raise their families.

Levites started their full-time ministry at age twenty-five and they continued in this role until age fifty. At this point in time, they were given financial security for the rest of their lives. They were still welcome to serve in God's house, but only if they wanted to. In my mind, this ranks as one of the best retirement plans in the world! The Lord God was serious about caring for His Levite servants from birth, right through to the end of their lives.

As the Levites made up one complete tribe of Israel, the ratio of Levites to regular people was one to twelve. In today's language, with a church congregation of three hundred people, it would work out to a staff of more than twenty full time, competitively paid workers!

Words to Levites

At this time, I would like to take a brief portage from our worship journey, and say a few personal words to my fellow Levites. I do this for two reasons—to encourage any set apart ones who might be reading, and also to help those who might be trying to understand an artistic worshiper who is close to them.

If you are a Levite, there is little you can do to escape your destiny. You are an individual who has a seal on your heart. You were born to serve in the house of the Lord. Your longings to worship, create, and work among God's people will be rooted so deeply inside your soul that you may be unable to discern where they end, and where you begin.

Positions such as leading worship, singing, playing instruments, technical directing, sound, media, film making, recording, graphics, prophetic painting, dance, drama, banners, writing, and artistic expressions of all kinds—these are not just things that we Levites do. They are callings entrenched in us from birth.

You might be a church leader, pastor, or children's director. I have a Levite friend who is an administrative assistant at a church. Her giftings are perfectly suited to what she does. She loves her community, serving them tirelessly. I have another acquaintance who is a custodian in God's house. The sincere way in which she cleans windows and vacuums carpets is truly remarkable. If you are called to serve in the house of the Lord, you are a Levite.

What do we do with such a grand calling? We take it seriously. This is not just a casual endeavor. It is every bit as essential as those original sacrifices out in the wilderness. We are part of an order ordained by God. We work hard to hone our skills so we can contribute with excellence. When our shift comes in God's house, we serve with humility, doing our part to the very best of our abilities. We also honor the various skill levels and demographics that we are teamed up with, laying down our right to perfection for the greater purpose of the pursuit of God's glory.

Longevity

In my travels, I rarely find people who thrive for long periods of time as a Levite. As I have been blessed to serve in this field for a lifetime, I would like to share a few things that have been keys to longevity for me.

Recreationally, I never let myself listen to music that is more than a couple of years old. I am relentless about keeping myself absolutely current on each instrument that I play. I constantly study and apply myself to current vocal, instrumental, and songwriting styles with all types of music.

There are dozens of different worship forms that these words apply to. If you are a dancer, persist in exploring cutting edge trends. If you are an artist, experiment with new medium and colors. Are you a public speaker? Stay up to date on language and nuance of expression. Whatever God has put in your heart, refuse to stay at the level you are at. Continue to improve and move forward—always.

The Levites of the wilderness tabernacle were only allowed to serve professionally for twenty-five years, but I believe it is possible to contribute at a relevant level for much longer. It takes having the same will to stay current at age eighty as we had when we were in the prime of our craft. As

> *As a Levite, you are part of an order ordained by God*

long as the Lord gives me breath, I will continue to learn and explore because it honors God and His exhaustive creativity.

Of extreme importance is health and fitness. Take care of your body. It will serve you well in the long run. Staying clear of stress and learning how to live dependent on God's strength is vital for a Levite. Stress kills creativity and doing things on our own strength leads to burn out.

Another key is learning to forgive. There is nothing more career shortening for a Levite than a heart full of bitterness. Our calling does not give us the right to become entitled, artistically jaded, or cynical when misunderstood. With the leading of the Holy Spirit, there are many ways our giftings can find expression in a diverse world.

Identity

It is very easy for a person with a strong life's calling to mistake it for his or her identity. I have fallen into this trap on many occasions. I have a Levite friend who was out for a walk one day talking with Jesus, when He spoke these words to her: "Don't ask me about what I have called you to do, instead ask me who I have created you to be."

In response, my question is, "Who are we?" Are we a singer, an artist, a worship leader? Or, are we a son, a daughter, and the object of God's affection? If we put our identity in our calling, we are setting ourselves up for a fall. By contrast, if our identity is rooted in the fact that we are loved by the Father, we will thrive. You are *first* a son and a daughter, created for intimacy and face-to-face time with Him. Let everything else related to your calling be a distant second.

> *We are first sons and daughters, created for intimacy and face-to-face time with Him*

Burnout

Sensitive and creative souls are often more susceptible to burnout than other personality types. Personally, I need to be deliberate about recharging myself in order to stay content and productive. An artistic person is not an infinite river of inspiration. It is impossible to churn out endless months of fresh creativity without a slow descent into the lower half of the creative barrel. Once you reach the bottom, it will take months, even years to heal.

A healthy work/life balance is non-negotiable for a Levite. Never let others put you in a position of doing too much or, even worse, turning out creativity like a machine. Somewhere down the line, there will be a price to pay. I have learned to recognize certain warning signs in my own life. The first thing I notice is a low level of resentment starting to build up. If I ignore this signal, other more serious signs will follow until I am forced to withdraw. At this point, I know there will be a long recovery time.

> *Above all else, guard your heart, for everything you do flows from it.*

> (Proverbs 4:23 NIV)

God has given you an incredible gift to which no earthly value can be assigned. Treat it with respect, and it will be a source of delight for years to come.

I Don't Get You

There have been many times in my life where I have been taken advantage of and misunderstood. I have noticed that some of the most hurtful situations can be brought on by those closest to us—a family member, a trusted friend, or even a spouse. It is difficult to explain the depth of calling that resides inside the heart of a Levite to someone who hasn't experienced the same thing.

It is important to be patient but firm in these moments. There might not be any easy answers as to why we react in certain ways, or care about things that don't seem to matter to others. I find it best to answer softly and then proceed through life with humility, integrity, and kindness. In the end, not everybody will "get you," but talk to Jesus—He will always understand and be on your side.

Give it Away

There is one more important aspect of being a Levite. Always be prepared to give what you have away. Never allow insecurity to creep into your heart when someone comes along who is more skilled than you. Give, give, and give. Pour into people even when it appears to threaten your position. Completely replace yourself if you can. You will never outgive God. Even in a worst-case scenario, He will have a fresh, new beginning prepared for you somewhere else—an even better place than where you are now.

To "Minister"

There is a phrase that is worth highlighting when it comes to what we Levites are called to do. It is the phrase "to minister." This word is used many times in Old Testament writings when referring to the Levites and it simply means to serve. We can minister directly to God, to each other, and to the lost of our world.

Out of these dimensions, the highest calling is to minister to the Lord Himself. Think of the God of this universe and how He created all things. Now imagine being given the task of serving Him personally and directly. It is a job reserved for the angels, and for those of us who have been called as Levites. When we minister to the Lord first, He responds, blessing us with His presence. It is out of this presence that we, in turn, minister to each other, and reach out to our world.

A Prayer

To close out this chapter, I would like to say a prayer over those readers who are Levites. You will know who you are. Please place your hand on your heart:

Father God, your callings are so beautiful. I am here before You, lifting up each person who has their hand on their heart right now. I pray that you will fill them with Your fullness. I pray they will hear Your song over them, that You will encounter them, and they will comprehend Your vast love for them. I am asking for protection and healing to be released over their sensitive, artistic souls. I am also asking that creativity be unleashed in them like they have never known before. Download for them new sounds, new songs, new dances, and new pictures. I pray that You would give them unusual favor for their journey.

But above all, I pray that You would bring them face to face with the light of the glory of Your countenance, Your presence, and Your goodness. Wreck them for all else I pray, in Jesus name.

Selah – pause in His presence

Chapter 6

DAVID AND THE ARK

Past the pages of Leviticus, Numbers, and Deuteronomy, we find the ark of the covenant taking on a progressively important role as a focal point of worship. The presence of God rested upon this strange looking box covered with gold. It was filled with such life that one of its contents, a branch, constantly budded. If the Levites are the caretakers of our house of worship, then the ark is its main piece of furniture and God's covering presence is the roof of the house.

Presence Encounters

A few years back, a couple of musician friends came to pay a visit to my office. We were talking about a worship night that we were going to host in a few days' time—looking through songs and discussing arrangements that might work in a more intimate setting with acoustic instruments. As we chatted, a sudden holy presence descended on our conversation. All three of us noticed it at the same time.

We waited in silence for a while. Then, one by one, we got down on our knees. Within a few minutes, our eyes began to fill with tears and our hearts started to burn with fire and wonder. A short time later, we were all on our faces. The presence lasted strong for forty-five minutes. When it finally lifted, we were so undone that we crawled out of the office—too weak to even walk. We have often talked about the time when, together, we were wrecked by the presence of Jesus.

Practice . . . Or?

For several years, I worked at a local bible college, teaching in the worship program. One afternoon, I was rehearsing with a group of students for the next morning's chapel. We were practicing a simple song of adoration—one that a student had written. As we began to tag the chorus, we felt the presence of Jesus descend on our practice space. We sang for a while longer, but the presence was so persistent that eventually we had to stop.

One at a time, we put down our instruments and sat on the floor. As we did, the presence settled into the atmosphere until we were all lying face down in a posture of worship, so overcome that we scarcely knew where we were. We never did finish our rehearsal that day. As a worship band, we stayed in that holy environment for over ninety minutes in a posture of awe and surrender.

Conference Glory Ball

A short while ago, I was at a large prophetic conference. On the final evening, the worship time was unusually anointed. During the third song, the worship leader recognized a shift in the atmosphere and began to press in to the moment. When she did, the presence of God filled the room until the space became charged with what almost felt like electricity.

The seating was limited. I was standing shoulder-to-shoulder with people on my right and left. In the crowded space, I still managed to raise my hands toward heaven but they were straight up rather than open wide. As I focused on heaven, several small feathers materialized in the air above me. After a while, I closed my eyes and began pouring out my heart in unrestrained worship.

A few minutes later I opened my eyes again and there, to my surprise, was a glowing, translucent ball of glory resting in my outstretched hands. It was about the size of a soccer ball. I bounced it from one hand to the other for a while and then sat down because my knees were too weak to stand any longer. When I did, the ball floated down and landed in my hands again. It stayed with me for almost thirty minutes as the worship continued.

Eventually the worship came to a close and when it did, the ball gradually disappeared. Over the next couple of weeks, from time to time I would see it again—sometimes during the day, or at night when it was dark. In the presence, there are always surprises. There is no telling what might happen!

Santa Really?

It was early Christmas morning a couple of years back when I had another beautiful encounter. I woke up at five-thirty a.m. to find the atmosphere of my room saturated with the presence of Jesus. I didn't understand why—there was no logical reason that I could tell, but I began to worship and pray in the spirit. As I did, the presence increased until I was thoroughly wrecked. I began drifting in and out of sleep as the encounter continued—it came in wave after wave.

At one point, the eyes of my heart were opened and I saw into the spirit world. An angel entered the room and put a small wrapped gift into my left hand, topped with a bright red bow. I opened it up to find a golden key inside, the type that would fit into a classic type of lock. As I fell in and out of consciousness, the Holy Spirit began to speak to me about new doors that the key would unlock as the future unfolded. The presence was with me for three solid hours. It was an unusual and rare Christmas gift that I received that morning, one I will treasure for years to come.

> *Just like the cloud in the desert, the presence of God is constantly on the move*

Psalm 23

Several years ago, my wife went out of town for the weekend with some friends. I was looking forward to doing a whole list of guy things with my time. However, after I dropped her off at the airport, I sat down with my bible and I heard the Holy Spirit prompt me to read the twenty-third psalm. Upon reading it through, I heard once again, "Read the twenty-third psalm." After the second pass through, I heard the Holy Spirit say, "You are not listening! I want you to read the twenty-third psalm all weekend long!"

I sat there stunned for a moment as I tried to come to grips with how I could read such a familiar portion of scripture for an entire weekend. That night and the next day, I made my best attempt at reading Psalm 23 over and over again. Eventually, I took out multiple bible translations and started looking up words in Hebrew lexicons. By the end of my reading marathon I was delirious with the thought of sheep, rods, and staffs.

The next morning, I had a few hours before heading off to pick my wife up from the airport so I sat down with my bible again. The same persistent whisper that I heard the first night came back to me, "Read the twenty-third psalm." I read it through once, twice, and was starting in for the third time when the presence of God suddenly filled the room. It hit me so strong that when I finally looked around, I found myself on the floor—weeping and disoriented.

In an instant, I had a profound download of the shepherd's heart of Jesus. I had an open vision of Psalm 23 before my eyes and I felt how He cares for His flock. I also knew that this same heart was now mine to carry for the people He would put in my pathway. The presence of the great Shepherd saturated me for almost two full hours that morning, forever changing my life and my perspective.

Selah – pause in His presence

A Quest for the Presence

I share the above stories because they are random. They range from unlikely meetings with friends, to worship gatherings—from personal encounters, to the word of God, and school rehearsals. The presence of God is not always found in the same place. Just like the cloud in the desert, it is constantly on the move and we as God's people are wise to move with it. Because of this steady shifting, those on a quest for the presence can never fall into comfortable patterns. The presence of God is always at the leading edge of the directions of the Spirit.

Here are some of the many places I have encountered the presence of God. I have discovered it in the love of God—to know God's love is to know His presence. I have found it at corporate gatherings of God's people and at parties. I have also experienced it by taking communion, reading God's word, waiting, dancing, and creating things. I have felt it while spirit soaking, resting, praying (in the natural or in the spirit), while with friends, while at work, in nature, in play, in laughter, and in worship.

I have learned that there is no way to use the presence of God to my advantage. It carries its own agenda, one set by God himself. If we try to use it for our purposes, it will leave and not come back.

It is also important to properly steward encounters with God's presence. Treat them as gifts—they are precious. Many times they are given as seeds for future breakthroughs, or as strength for a specific journey. It is never wrong to watch for further confirmation on something you have seen, or to ask the Holy Spirit for clarity on something that has happened. I highly recommend journaling, praying, and waiting as ways to decompress experiences with the presence.

The Ark Goes for a Field Trip

The ark of the covenant took a forty-year journey through the wilderness. It was a very heavy little treasure chest and it was saturated with God's presence inside and out. Some have estimated it to weigh over four hundred pounds. Whenever the cloud began to move, it was lifted up and carried on the shoulders of the priests, sometimes for hours. There was an ancient Hebrew saying that, "the Levites didn't carry the ark, the ark carried them."

The ark existed for its own purposes. It was utterly holy. On a few occasions, several individuals got into serious trouble for trying to offer up unholy sacrifices or for using the ark in ways not sanctioned by the Law of Moses. God's presence will not be dishonored or manipulated for human gain.

It eventually found a permanent resting place when the Israelites took possession of their promised land. The wilderness tabernacle was set up permanently on a hill in a place called Gibeon. The ark was placed inside the holy of holies and the sacrifices of worship continued in a fixed location. The tabernacle and the ark stayed there all the way through the era of the judges.

> *I have learned that there is no way to use the presence of God to my advantage*

On one occasion, God's people were faced with a dreadful war against the Philistines. Out of fear, the Israeli army generals decided to take the ark out of the tabernacle to the front lines of the battle in hopes that it would give them a victory. Instead, the ark was captured and taken to a foreign land.

What the Philistines thought would be a prized spoil of war soon became a source of great consternation for them. The presence of God that rested upon the ark knocked down their idols and caused them no end of grief.

After a few months, the Philistines decided that they wanted nothing more to do with the ark so they put it on a cart pulled by two young cows and sent it down the road. The cows randomly pulled the ark back toward the land of Israel. Once it crossed the homeland border, some very curious people decided to try and open up the ark to see what was inside. Sadly, their disrespect for God's presence cost them their lives and the ark was left abandoned on a rock where it rested for a while. Then it was taken to a farmhouse where it stayed for years, and there a priest cared for it.

> *The presence of God is the only thing that makes worship alive*

It is in this setting that we first find the term, "Ichabod." It is a Hebrew word that means "no glory," For several decades, the people of Israel attempted to worship without the glory and presence of God. It was an extremely dark time in the history of God's people, lasting up until king David brought the ark back to Jerusalem.

I often wonder how much time we spend trying to worship with no glory. My heart breaks when I find myself in a worship gathering where form and religion has replaced the glory of God. I have noticed that many times the worshipers aren't even aware that the glory is absent.

I have seen people sit through services with angry hearts

because the worship wasn't done to their liking. I have experienced worship reduced to formula, with rote substituting for God's presence. I have also seen worshipers relegated to the place of a warm up act, forcing them into performance and crowd prep mode, paving the way for a slick service transition.

If we are scrutinizing the worship in our gatherings, looking for fault, critiquing worship theology, and analyzing worship leaders who are honestly trying to be led by the Holy Spirit, then we have not come to worship at all. We have come to be entertained and to consume. There is no glory in this kind of an offering.

The presence of God is the only thing that makes worship alive. Without it there is no fire and the offering is "Ichabod," devoid of the glory. A sacrifice left unconsumed, like the offering that Cain tried to bring, eventually turns rancid, resulting in death rather than life.

Presence filled worship is not difficult to enter into. It requires one thing—that we lay down our agenda and embrace the Holy Spirit's timing as He leads us to the Father. Worship is not ours. It is His. We don't get to define it, He does. We don't get to have it the way we want; it is all about Him.

David – A Man of the Presence

King David was a person who had great respect for the presence of God. He also carried a crazy fascination for the ark of the covenant. Many of his early psalms express the desire to be in God's house—beholding the beauty, majesty, and glory of the Lord. He was the youngest child in a large family and he became known as a "man after God's own heart."

When we first see David in the bible, he is a teenager tending his father's sheep. He was a musician who filled his time playing his harp, writing songs, and worshiping. His musical skill was so renowned that he was eventually asked by the king to come and play at the royal palace. This would have been a great honor for any musician, similar to an invitation to go and perform at the White House.

David's journey from shepherd boy to king produced some of the most celebrated stories in the bible. However, it is David's heart for worship that sets him apart as one of the most significant persons to ever live.

A Pattern of the Presence

As a young Jewish boy, David would have made periodic visits to the tabernacle with his family to bring sacrifices before the Lord. I imagine him watching with wide-eyed wonder as God's presence filled the atmosphere at the temple.

Over the course of time, David clearly started to recognize a pattern. He learned that the same presence rested on him at the tabernacle as when he sat out in those pastures singing to the Lord. This connection eventually led him to change the expression of worship for his generation. David also learned that it wasn't really a blood sacrifice that God was after—it was the sacrifice of the heart:

> *Unseal my lips, O Lord, that my mouth may praise you. You do not desire a sacrifice, or I would offer one. You do not want a burnt offering. The sacrifice you desire is a broken spirit. You will not reject a broken and repentant heart, O God.*

> (Psalms 51:15-17)

Once David became king, one of the first things he did was devise a plan to bring the treasure of worship—the ark, back to Jerusalem. His first attempt failed, but the second time David was successful. The ark made a celebrated return back to the royal city resting on the shoulders of the Levites, just as in the days of the wilderness journey.

Put the Ark Where?

The holy of holies was a small sanctuary inside the tabernacle. Up until the ark was captured, it had always rested in this inner room along with a set of cherubim and a few other choice pieces of furniture. However, when David brought the ark back to Jerusalem, he didn't put it back where it belonged. Instead, he opted for something altogether different. Perhaps this was a

> *David's heart for worship sets him apart as one of the most significant persons to ever live*

childhood dream of his, something he imagined while out tending sheep. It was so compelling that he danced in the streets as the ark entered the city gates.

David changed the course of history by bringing the ark of the presence to a place called Mount Zion instead of returning it to the Gibeon tabernacle. He then placed it inside a new tent that he had constructed to house God's glory.

This was an extremely bold move on David's part. The ark was not something to be messed with. It was an object shrouded in mystery, created as the centerpiece of the holy of holies. The rules for its handling and placement were specific and restrictive. Its purpose was intertwined with the sacrifices of God's people, the remission of sin, and the law— and it was now miles away from its home. But what David did next is even more brazen. He put musicians and singers inside his new tent to worship before the ark day and night.

I am completely bemused at the random logic that would take the most holy piece of tabernacle furniture, separate it from its home, place it in an unknown tent, and make people sing in front of it! However, David was so confident in his relationship with the God of the presence from the sheep fields, that he acted with fearlessness.

> *Worship in front of the ark was very multigenerational*

Meanwhile, the blood sacrifices kept taking place at the Gibeon tabernacle, but it was now arkless. The presence no longer rested there—it had been moved and the new sacrifice was now the sound of thanksgiving, praise, and musical worship.

This new structure of worship lasted for forty years, well into king Solomon's reign.

Selah – pause in His presence

A New Order of Worship

Thankfully, God was pleased to listen to the new offerings of praise and worship and accept it as an alternative to the blood sacrifices that had been at the center of worship for thousands of years.

King David, the man after God's own heart, took a huge, calculated risk. As a reward, he was blessed with something that no other person under the law had ever been given—a window of access to what worship would look like after the cross, which we enjoy today!

Once the ark was in its new resting place, an elaborate system of Levitical worship was set up by David. The story of the Zion worship community is well documented in the books of 1 Chronicles and 2 Samuel. Here are some of the details of the new order of worship, how it worked, and some of the people who were involved.

There were three main Levites assigned by David to care for the worship in front of the ark. Their names were Asaph, Heman, and Jeduthun.

Asaph was the chief musician and he was a drummer— yes, you read correctly! In a couple of places, it mentions that Asaph's specialty was to play the loud sounding cymbals, tambourines, and castanets. His sons were also musicians.

Heman was a seer and a musician. His sons and daughters were also musicians, lyre players, harpists, and singers.

Jeduthun along with his family were harpists. The bible tells us they prophesied with their harps in thanksgiving and praise to the Lord. (1 Chronicles 25:3)

Asaph was in charge of scheduling, leading, and shepherding the worship teams who played around the ark day and night. The scriptures state that there were 288 skilled singers and musicians left to minister to the Lord in the presence! (1 Chronicles 25:7) The very next verse reveals that they cast lots for their places on the worship roster, the small and great, the teacher and pupil alike. Worship in front of the ark was multi-generational—many different ages and skill levels were represented. A culture of honor existed where new creative worshipers were constantly being mentored into the worship experience alongside the seasoned ones.

There were also recorders. These individuals would sit in the presence of the ark and document everything that happened. It is from this practice that we get many of our psalms. They originated as spontaneous worship in front of the ark, the recorders wrote them down, and some of them made it into our bible. I used to wonder why I had such a love for recording and producing music. Once I learned of these individuals, it all made sense to me.

The Ark-Tent

I would like for us to imagine what this all must have looked like. On a hill in central Jerusalem sat a brand-new tent. This worship center was situated on Mount Zion, a place formerly known as Mount Moriah, the location of Abraham's sacrifice of Isaac. Inside the tent was the ark of the covenant. The Levites would enter the tent in shifts and bring their worship before the Lord.

The ark was saturated and surrounded by the presence of God, so the worship was done in the glory and toward the ark. This was not a worship band facing a congregation concert style and leading people in the singing of songs. Instead, think of the worshipers facing the ark and ministering directly to the Lord Himself. There was nothing to gain adrenaline from. There was no applause from which to draw energy. There were just the worshipers—and the ark.

Chapter 7

JUST YOU AND THE ARK

You have been invited on a journey. You are part of David's Zion worshiping community. You are a lyre player.

It is Monday night and you have drawn the 2-5 a.m. shift in your weekly lot. You arrive at the Zion ark-tent at 1:47 a.m., unwrap your instrument, and get it tuned up in anticipation for the hand off from the previous worship shift. As you wait in the corridor, you bow your head, quieting your heart, bringing all of the cares of the day and surrendering them one by one. This is the presence of Almighty God you will be entering in a few minutes—it is not a place for distractions. It is a most holy environment. This is true and pure servanthood. The night air is cold and there are no modern conveniences, no green room, no Evian water, and no red Smarties (as specified in your rider) waiting for you.

There will be no crowd to listen to your praises tonight. There will be no sound check, no tech rehearsal, and no in-ear monitors. It will be just you, your worship team, and the ark. If the presence of God is not there, it will be a long, sleepless night. However, in the presence, this could very well be the most exciting three hours you have ever spent as a worshiper. The following saying could very well be true: "Better is one day (or even one hour) in Your house than a thousand elsewhere."

Zion Worship Guidelines

Now let's break from our imagination for a moment. I would like to highlight a few important things about the ark-tent to set a context for our journey.

At Zion, there was no audience. The only focus of attention was the ark and the Lord Himself. I have often heard a saying that worship should be before an "audience of one." In the ark-tent, this was truly the case.

At Zion, the specific job of the musicians was to minister to the Lord (1 Chronicles 16:4). In our modern-day worship culture, far too often, I have experienced trying to get people into the worship, warmed up, and over their week before turning our attention toward Jesus. In the ark-tent, it was all about Him from the very first note.

At Zion, worship was the main event. There was no precedent for using the worship as a precursor for the ensuing offering and sermon. In the ark-tent, it was worship and only worship.

At Zion, the presence of God was central to the worship experience. If the presence was not there, worship was an exercise in futility. God's presence can so subtly be substituted for many things such as crowd energy, adrenaline, buzz enhanced by a good sound and lighting system, and even participation as far as people singing loudly. All of these things, if not clearly discerned, can give a false sense of atmosphere in a room that can masquerade as a counterfeit for the presence of God. God's glory alone must be central to worship.

There is a bible passage I would like for us to look at briefly. It will help lay a scriptural foundation for our imagination.

> *David appointed the following Levites to lead the people in worship before the ark of the Lord—to invoke his blessings, to give thanks, and to praise the Lord, the God of Israel. Asaph, the leader of this group, sounded the cymbals. Second to him was Zechariah, followed by Jeiel, Shemiramoth, Jehiel, Mattithiah, Eliab, Benaiah, Obed-edom, and Jeiel. They played the harps and lyres. The priests, Benaiah and Jahaziel, played the trumpets regularly before the ark of God's covenant.*

(1 Chronicles 16:4-6)

The Hand Off

While waiting for the early morning shift to begin, you glance at the schedule posted beside the door and notice that tonight, the musicians and singers will be joined by a group of worship dancers and a group of Levite ladies who specialize in waving banners around the ark. There is also a four-

> *God's presence can subtly be substituted for many things*

teen-year-old boy who paints mosaics on large papyrus sheets, as well as a young Levite woman who loves to create multicolored blankets of cloth. She will be weaving her art in front of the ark tonight.

Your focus is broken as the musicians from the previous shift make their way out of the ark-tent. They seem excited. One of them mentions to you that the glory is extra strong tonight. A young Levite singer seems to stagger as she comes out of the door, almost too overcome to stand on her own. The others rush to her side, helping her out into the night air—laughing as they go.

As you enter the tent, you see the ark sitting off to the side. There is a visible glow that surrounds the ark tonight— the Shekinah of God. The way it radiates always takes you by surprise because it can look different on any given shift. It seems even more beautiful tonight than you remembered from last week.

The women begin unwrapping their banners. The dancers begin warming up in the pre-shift silence, preparing the atmosphere, inviting the Lord of Creation to reveal Himself in a whole new way tonight. The young Levite woman who loves to weave is laying her supplies out on the ground, just off to the side of the ark. You notice the various strands of thread and gold as they glitter in the light of the glory. The boy is unfolding a large stretched rack with a papyrus sheet attached to it along with his colors and painting sticks.

As you look around the tent, you are reminded of a song that was written a few months ago specifically to honor the night shift worshipers.

Psalm 134

Title: Praising the Lord in His House at Night – A Song of Ascents

Oh, praise the Lord, all you servants of the Lord
You who serve at night in the house of the Lord
Lift your hands toward the sanctuary and praise the Lord
May the Lord, who made heaven and earth bless you from
Jerusalem

Your Shift Begins

Tonight, you and your worship team will be starting things off with a well-known song. It was written a few years ago in a moment of spontaneous worship in front of the ark and thankfully, the very diligent worship recorders documented it. They sit off to the left and right side of the ark just waiting for moments such as these. It has since become a classic and one of your favorite songs.

Psalm 150

Title: A Psalm of Praise

Praise the Lord!
Praise God in his sanctuary;
Praise him in his mighty heaven!
Praise him for his mighty works;
Praise his unequaled greatness!
Praise him with a blast of the ram's horn;
Praise him with the lyre [that's you!] *and harp!*
Praise him with the tambourine and dancing;
Praise him with strings and flutes!

> *Praise him with a clash of cymbals;*
> *Praise him with loud clanging cymbals.*
> *Let everything that breathes sing praises to the Lord!*
> *Praise the Lord!*

Your lyre springs to life as you join the ensemble, bringing praise and thanksgiving to the God of heaven and earth. The banner artists begin lifting up their colored flags high on poles and waving them in layered patterns over the ark. Each banner has a different Hebrew phrase sewn into it. Some contain words of praise like Hallah and Yadah. Others have colored emblems and worship slogans. As the banners pass over the ark, you notice it is creating an effect almost like fanning the flames of a fire. The Shekinah glory is swirling around in the wind created by the movement of the flags. As it does, it seems to increase in intensity with each passing song verse.

As the musicians and the choir move on to the second song, the banner wavers step to the side of the ark-tent and start to walk slowly around the edges of the worship hall. As they do, the dancers take their place around the ark. They are doing a dance called the Machowl—a traditional Jewish circle dance. At this point, you notice the glory of God changing colors. Sometimes it looks almost golden. The next moment, it appears sapphire blue. It seems to shift from one end of the spectrum to the next as you continue to praise and exalt the name of the Lord.

The choir tonight is made up of a dozen individuals of different ages and vocal ranges. They stand on a platform made of cedar that faces the ark from the left side. At times they sing as a group. Other times they sing answering stanzas in the songs, alternating between male and female vocal parts. Each song is arranged by Asaph, the Zion worship co-ordinator, to fit the style and range of the vocalists. The choir director is dressed in a robe that seems to constantly catch the light waves that stream from the ark.

The music ensemble sits on the other side of the ark. Tonight, there are eight musicians including yourself. There is a duo of flutists, a trumpeter, a percussionist, and a group playing various types of stringed instruments like lyres and harps. Every shift in front of the ark has a slightly different musical feel because the Levites always pick their spots on the schedule by drawing lots. It is a constant pleasure to find out who you are teamed up with on any given shift.

Tonight, it seems as if time stands still in the presence of the ark. The songs are now alternating between giving thanks and praise, and you notice a cloud of glory starting to enve-lope the room. It appears first on the ground as wisps of smoke. Then it slowly starts to rise and fill the atmosphere.

With the addition of this manifestation of the Shekinah, you notice that the glory is becoming almost too strong for the dancers to continue on their feet. Many of them are now on their knees before the ark. This action embodies the true essence of the Hebrew word Barak. It means to "kneel in praise."

You glance over toward the young man who is busy with his papyrus sheet. At this point in his artistic process, it seems like he is creating layer upon layer of color in a sweeping motion, almost like the ocean surf. It is at this time that you notice a shift in the room. As the environment moves toward worship, wave upon wave of glory sweeps through the atmosphere. It appears to mirror the action of the boy and his painting sticks as he pushes his colors from one side of his parchment to the other.

The banner wavers are bowing before the Lord of the ark now, their banners laid out in front of them in a display of reverence and awe. They are offering up verbal praise to the God of Israel shouting out, "Holy, Holy, Holy is the Lord Jehovah." The dancers answer them, raising their hands toward heaven and declaring, "Blessing and honor and power to the Father of Creation."

You notice one young dancer who is somehow still on her feet. She steps into the area in front of the ark and does a series of pirouettes and other graceful moves that leave you breathless. With every step she seems to attract more presence and glory into the room. Eventually she bows down and lays prostrate before the ark in a posture of worship, the glory of God overcoming her.

The pre-planned worship set is coming to a close but the worship isn't over. What comes next is your favorite part of the entire shift—the spontaneous worship segment. The musicians and singers start pairing up now. Each pair begins to take their turn, singing and playing new songs from their hearts in front of the ark. The songs begin in a simple way, repeating just a few words and chords over and over again. Then the entire worship ensemble joins in to enhance the creative process as the songs start to take shape, flowing from moments of glory to glory.

Tonight, you have been paired together with one of the baritone singers. He suddenly catches a divine inspiration of glory and begins to sing a new song to the Lord. You follow his melody line with your lyre, laying down a simple chord pattern and rhythm for him to sing along with. Within a few moments, you, together with your entire ensemble, are creating a beautiful new song, spontaneously flowing from nuance to nuance as if it had been planned from the beginning.

You notice the two recorders frantically dipping their pens in their inkwells and writing on the parchments in front of them. One of them records the lyrics of the song while the other one documents the melody and the chord structure. Later on, they will combine their efforts into one master chart containing the finished song, which will then be passed on to the chief worship leader, Asaph.

Once your new song is finished, your eye is drawn to the side of the ark, to the young woman who has been weaving her artistic tapestry all night long. Her cloth creation is now several feet wide, multicolored, and exceptionally beautiful. She has somehow woven fine strands of gold into the fabric and it is catching the glow from the ark, casting diamond-like sparkles of glory light all around the room. She is lifting it toward heaven, waving it slowly in front of the ark.

You are utterly lost in the moment. The glory of God is so strong that it is almost impossible for anyone to stand—almost everyone is bowing in worship before the presence of

God and the ark now. You and a few members of your band do your best to stay in your places to provide a musical backdrop for the worship. All eyes are on the ark, all minds are on the Lord God of Israel, and all hearts are swimming in a pool of wonder and awe.

As you look around, it becomes evident what the young man with the papyrus rack was creating. He has painted an

> *This is what you were created for—to offer up thanks, praise, and worship in the presence of the glory of the Lord*

artisanal mosaic of the Sea of Kinneret, a lake in the north country that you have visited a few times. He has pushed the waves of the water into golden colored peaks around a shoreline that is punctuated with bulrushes and reeds. The Shekinah accentuates the waves, making them seem alive with action and movement.

The cloud of glory has almost filled the entire room now. It is radiant but somehow translucent, all at the same time. Every time you take a breath in this atmosphere, you feel a warmth fill your entire body. Every now and again, you notice a lightning-like flash of glory proceeding from the area just above the ark. You recall the comment from your friend before your shift started, how the glory was extra strong tonight. He was definitely not exaggerating!

You and your entire worship ensemble are scattered out over the floor area—some are on their knees, some face down, some sitting. Everyone is soaking in the presence, waiting on the God of all glory. No one dares to talk. There is not a dry eye to be found anywhere in the room.

Out of one ear you hear a rustling in the hallway outside. It must be the worship team for the next shift getting ready to take over from where your group has left off. You wonder at where the time has gone. Three hours has only seemed like a few minutes. The presence of God in the tent is so indescribably beautiful that it will be difficult to tear yourself away from this atmosphere, but there is always tomorrow to look forward to.

As you and your friends finally make your way out of the ark-tent, you wonder at the strong Shekinah tonight. There is no place you would rather be. Deep in your Levite's heart you know that this is what you were created for—to offer up thanks, praise, and worship in the presence of the glory of the Lord!

Tonight, your dreams will be sweet—and your next shift is only twenty-one hours away!

Selah – pause in His presence

ENCOUNTERED *in* WORSHIP

Chapter 8

THE ARK RETURNS HOME

In my travels, I often run across people who have never heard of David's ark-tent or the 24/7 Zion Levitical community. There are many scriptures that describe this continuous worship ministry.

> *So He* [David] *left Asaph and his relatives there before the ark of the covenant of the Lord to minister before the ark continually.*

(1 Chronicles 16:37 NASB)

Worship in front of the ark began when David put the ark inside the tent and it continued through the rest of his kingly reign. The Levites spent thousands of hours in God's presence inside that humble tent—a structure that eventually became known as the "tabernacle of David."

Soon after that time, David started a campaign to build a permanent temple for the presence of the Lord, but God stopped him. God told David that He had no desire for a lofty house of cedar—that He was quite happy in a tent. He then relented, telling David that his son, Solomon, would build the temple.

Why Not David?

I have often wondered why God prevented David from building the temple. The bible states it was because he was a

> David led a whole generation into the presence of the Lord

man of bloodshed and war, but at times, I wonder if something else was going on in the heart of God. It was no secret that eventually the ark of the covenant would need to be returned to the veiled holy of holies and reunited with the cherubim, but could it be that God longed to be face-to-face with His worshipers for just a few extra years?

David, however, was undaunted. Even though God stopped him from building the temple, nothing could keep him from gathering together the supplies. He put considerable effort into collecting massive amounts of materials—wood, gold, silver, bronze, and iron for God's new house. Near the end of David's life, he called a national assembly and took an offering for the temple. Some have estimated the monetary value of this offering to be in the billions of dollars. After the offering, David prayed a prayer of blessing over the people of Israel. The prayer ended like this:

> And David said to all the assembly, "Now bless Jehovah your God." And all the assembly blessed Jehovah, the God of their fathers, and bowed down their heads, and worshiped Jehovah, and the king.

(1 Chronicles 29:20 ASV)

I see an entire kingdom of people who had learned to worship in this verse. David, the sweet minstrel of Israel, led a whole generation into the presence of the Lord and taught them the true value of worship and the glory of God.

Solomon Takes Over

When Solomon took over as king, worship in the ark-tent continued for several more years as the new temple was being built. This lofty structure was constructed to replace both the wilderness tabernacle on Mount Gibeon, and David's ark-tent. Like the wilderness tabernacle, it had an outer court, an inner court, and also a holy of holies.

The commissioning of the new temple was a massive civic event. It began with a passionate prayer of dedication by king Solomon and the celebrations lasted for two full weeks. Almost a half century after being taken out to battle, the ark was finally home.

When Solomon finished praying, fire flashed down from heaven and burned up the burnt offerings and sacrifices, and the glorious presence of the Lord filled the temple. The priests could not enter the temple of the Lord because the glorious presence of the Lord filled it. The priests took their assigned positions, and so did the Levites who were singing, "His faithful love endures forever!" They accompanied the singing with music from the instruments king David had made for praising the Lord. Across from the Levites, the priests blew the trumpets, while all Israel stood.

(2 Chronicles 7:1-2,6)

After this event, worship resumed in the manner of the Law of Moses. Sacrifices were made on the altar in front of the new temple and the priests went in once a year to sprinkle blood on the ark. Once it was placed inside the holy of holies, the Levites no longer worshiped in front of the ark. They now played in the inner court.

Once the temple was dedicated, God appeared to Solomon in a dream. These were His words:

> *As for you, if you live in my presence as your father David lived, pure in heart and action, living the life I've set out for you, attentively obedient to my guidance and judgments, then I'll back your kingly rule over Israel, make it a sure thing on a solid foundation.*

(1 Kings 9:4-5 MSG)

The Hebrew translation of this verse reads: "If you will live before my 'face' (paneh) as did David your father." David was a man of the presence—he lived before the face of God. Solomon, on the other hand, when given a choice to ask for anything he wished, made his appeal for wisdom. Asking for wisdom was not a bad thing. In fact, it pleased God. However, wisdom outside of God's presence eventually degraded into mere knowledge and became a snare for the young king.

The Kingdom Darkens

As Solomon's reign continued, many subtle departures took place in Israel. Wealth and a strong sense of national security began to replace a reliance on God for safety and supply. Even though worship was done in front of the temple,

Solomon eventually started to worship in the high places of the country—places where there was no presence. This practice led to idolatry. The kingdom slowly slipped into a downward spiral and the values of worship that David had set up began to fade from the national consciousness.

There is one person I would like to mention during this time in the history of God's people. Asaph was alive during both David's and Solomon's reign. He was a young man when David left him in charge of the ark-tent worship, and according to biblical records, he lived a long life. He wrote numerous Psalms. Some were written during the time of David and the ark-tent, some during Solomon's era, and some later on in Solomon's reign when things had darkened in the kingdom of Israel.

Psalm 73 is an example of a psalm that Asaph wrote in his old age, long after the ark-tent worship had ceased. In Asaph's defense, to worship for years directly in front of the ark under a radical king, and then to see everything he loved change, erode, and eventually become lost must have been heartbreaking. Asaph witnessed foreigners and persons of violence defiling the tem-

> *Wisdom outside of the presence of God can eventually degrade into mere knowledge*

ple, destroying the very thing that had been most dear to him—the presence of God. In this passionate piece of poetry, he describes his bitterness over watching the decline. He also laments that life in the context of the sanctuary and God's presence is the only thing that brings him hope.

From Personal Experience

I can clearly relate to the disappointment that sets in when you have been in the presence of God, and then, when you enter a place where it isn't honored to the same degree that you are accustomed to. After worshiping in the presence, directly in front of the ark, nothing else compares; everything else seems empty. For those with a history of encounter and glory, it is difficult to go backward once you have experienced this kind of worship.

Several times in my life, I have been in environments so charged with the presence that I have been unable to stand. I have seen the cloud of God's glory visibly on occasion to the degree that I was absolutely lost in worship. Several hours later I came to my senses and wondered where the time had gone.

I have been in corporate worship services where the musicians and singers were worshiping, the dancers were dancing, the banners were waving, and art was being created. The glory of God has faithfully descended, leaving us all undone and wrecked.

> *True and pure worship is not a hot worship band and a room charged with audience buzz*

There have been times in my life that I have worked in places where the presence was given first priority. Then circumstances have changed, new leadership has assumed control, and God's presence has become a distant thought in the service planning meetings. I have also served in churches where form and tradition have held the first priority, doctrine trumping all things related to worship.

A few years ago, I was sifting through some church job listings when I came across the following description:

> Fifth Avenue Church [fictitious name] is searching for a new worship pastor. Must have rock star quality vocals, rock star quality lead instrument and song writing skills, and a rock star quality stage presence. We do not apologize for demanding high standards as seen from the world's perspective from our worship staff. Must also have experience directing Broadway quality musicals and have a thorough understanding of the most up-to-date lighting and visual media styles. Must be able to lead a creative team into the future with the latest cutting-edge trends and technology. We are looking for a person who will be the embodiment of our church values and vision statement. Please apply with your CV and demo videos at ...

As I read through the rest of the page, my eyes filled with tears and I said a silent prayer for this church and its leadership team.

God's people substitute so many things for the "one thing" when it comes to worship. True and pure worship is not a good sound system, a trendy song leader with spiky hair and skinny jeans, a hot band, or a room charged with audience buzz. I have heard the phrase, "There's a lot of love in this room," referring to the warm glow that a crowd of people can generate when gathered together. This is not the presence of God. It is a substitute.

In the ark-tent, there was no crowd to play to. It was just the worshipers and the ark—God's people and His presence. This is something that we desperately need to rediscover today. Only through full surrender to the leadership of the Holy Spirit can we enter that presence filled ark-tent once again.

Selah – pause in His presence

Heroes of Worship

In the years after Solomon's reign, Israel became divided and dark. Idol worship became commonplace as king after king led God's people far away from His heart. Yet even in the darkest of times, God has always had His remnant. I would like to pay tribute to a few outstanding Old Testament worshipers—people who worshiped even when faced with desperate circumstances.

Elijah Lights it Up

Elijah was a crazy worshiper. He once single handedly challenged over four hundred prophets of Baal to a worship showdown on Mount Carmel! The prophets of Baal worshiped all day long but Baal did not answer from heaven. Then Elijah built an altar at the time of the evening sacrifice and called on the name of the Lord. God's glory fire came down from heaven, consuming the sacrifice, and even the stones on the altar.

> *The gifts of prophecy and worship are closely and beautifully intertwined*

A Dynamic Combination

Elisha was a prophet of great power and distinction. Although he is best known for his many miracles, he was a worshiper who spent much of his life as a political activist. He lobbied tirelessly against corruption and idolatry. He was often hated by his own government for his stance against evil, but whenever they would get into a difficult situation, they would go looking for him.

On one occasion, the king of Israel was faced with a war. He began searching for a prophet to confirm whether or not he should go out to battle. Eventually, Elisha was brought before the king. Elisha asked for a Levite to accompany him as he prophesied.

> *"Now bring me someone who can play the harp." While the harp was being played, the power of the Lord came upon Elisha.*

(2 Kings 3:15)

Here we find the gift of prophecy and worship working in combination. These two gifts are closely and beautifully intertwined.

A Dedicated Priest

Jehoiada was a priest before the Lord during a very dark time in Judea's history. After a string of evil leadership turnovers and national tragedies, he decided to gather together the Levites and install a new king—Joash, who was only seven years old at the time. During the festivities, he called a great worship assembly.

> *The captains and the trumpeters were beside the king. And all the people of the land rejoiced and blew trumpets, the singers with their musical instruments leading the praise.*

(2 Chronicles 23:13 NASB)

After this event, Judea made a covenant with the Lord and the entire country went on a rampage, tearing down idols and removing all the altars of Baal. Jehoiada then began to restore the Levites and the worship of the temple.

> *Jehoiada now put the priests and Levites in charge of the Temple of the Lord, following all the directions given by David. He also commanded them to present burnt offerings to the Lord, as prescribed by the Law of Moses, and to sing and rejoice as David had instructed.*

(2 Chronicles 23:18)

In partnership with the young king, Joash, Jehoiada brought God's people back to a heart of worship for almost forty years.

Jehu Brings It

Jehu reigned as king for a period of twenty-eight years. He was zealous for the Lord and restored true worship to Israel. Because he succeeded a very wicked king/wife combination, Ahab and Jezebel, he inherited a country that was immersed in idolatry from top to bottom. Jehu went on a campaign to completely eradicate idol worship from his country. He destroyed all of the priests of Baal and tore down every idol he could find.

They dragged out the sacred pillar used in the worship of Baal and burned it. They smashed the sacred pillar and wrecked the temple of Baal, converting it into a public toilet, as it remains to this day. In this way, Jehu destroyed every trace of Baal worship from Israel.

(2 Kings 10:26-28)

Hezekiah Turns Hearts

I would like to honor Hezekiah, another Judean king. He shines brightly as one who brought God's people back to the heart of worship. He restored the temple and all the elements of worship, eventually calling a great assembly and making an elaborate sacrifice to the Lord. Along with the sacrifice, he restored the Levitical musicians and the prophets:

The king ordered the Levites to take their places in the temple of God with their musical instruments—cymbals, harps, zithers—following the original instructions of David. The Levites formed the orchestra of David, while the priests took up the trumpets. Then Hezekiah gave the signal to begin. The Whole-Burnt-Offering was offered on the altar. At the same time the sacred choir began singing, backed up by the trumpets and the David orchestra while the entire congregation worshiped. The singers sang and the trumpeters played all during the sacrifice of the Whole-Burnt-Offering. When the offering of the sacrifice was completed, the king and everyone there knelt to the ground and worshiped. Then Hezekiah the king and the leaders told the Levites to finish things off with anthems of praise to God using lyrics by David and Asaph the seer. They sang their praises with joy and reverence, kneeling in worship.

(2 Chronicles 29:25-30 MES)

During the age of the kings, there was no other person who did more to restore the worship of God's people than Hezekiah. He brought full time musicians back to the temple, replacing them in positions of honor and value in the spirit of David.

How Do You Pronounce Those Names Again?

There is another small group of outstanding worshipers—Daniel and his three friends Shadrach, Meshach, and Abednego. Daniel worshiped God faithfully three times a day. He would kneel down on his Jerusalem facing porch and pray, offering thanks and worship to God. He refused to stop praying even when faced with a decree that threatened to put him in a den of lions. Daniel was unstoppable in his worship and God delivered him from the lions. He was also a person who was given extraordinary prophetic insight.

Shadrach, Meshach, and Abednego were also dedicated worshipers. They stood alone in a field of thousands, defying a decree to bow down and worship a golden image. As the musicians of the day played to the crowd, driving them into a frenzy, the three friends refused to compromise their worship. This decision made the king so angry that he threw them into a fiery furnace—one so hot that it killed the men who tossed them in. When God saved them from the fire, the king was so filled with awe that he ordered a new decree:

> *The question since our earth was created has always been—whom will you worship?*

> *Nebuchadnezzar* [the king] *said, "Blessed be the God of Shadrach, Meshach, and Abednego! He sent his angel and*

rescued his servants who trusted in him! They ignored the king's orders and laid their bodies on the line rather than serve or worship any god but their own. "Therefore, I issue this decree: Anyone anywhere, of any race, color, or creed, who says anything against the God of Shadrach, Meshach, and Abednego will be ripped to pieces, limb from limb, and their houses torn down. There has never been a god who can pull off a rescue like this."

(Daniel 3:28-29 MES)

This trio of young worshipers brought about a reverse political decision given by a powerful pagan king just because of their dedication and worship to God.

In the end, there has really only been one battle down through the centuries of our human existence. The question since our earth was created has always been—whom will you worship?

Wise Worshipers

As we turn the pages of our bible to the New Testament, we find another memorable worship event. In Matthew's account of the birth of Jesus, wise men came to visit the newborn king:

About that time some wise men from eastern lands arrived in Jerusalem, asking, "Where is the newborn king of the Jews? We saw his star as it rose, and we have come to worship him." And the star they had seen in the east guided them to Bethlehem. It went ahead of them and stopped over the place where the child was. When they saw the star, they were filled with joy! They entered the house and saw the child with his mother, Mary, and they bowed down and worshiped him. Then they opened their treasure chests and gave him gifts of gold, frankincense, and myrrh.

(Matthew 2:1-2, 9-11 MES)

Described above is a classic version of "Shachah" worship. A group of men come in search of a king. When they find him, the first thing they do is bow down in worship. They take out gifts, which they present to the newborn king as an act of homage. Their worship was a combination of surrender, respect, reverence, and bringing what was due. The wise men undoubtedly understood the Hebrew word for "worship" and they followed this ancient activity with precision.

Down through the centuries, these worshipers and many others whose names aren't mentioned in the bible, set their eyes on God and His presence even when everyone else ridiculed them. They stood alone, fought battles, defied rulers, took kingdom ground, made sacrifices, and gave up their lives all while on their knees, bowed low in worship. In the end, their crown will be everlasting and unfading—the crown of glory.

Selah – pause in His presence

Chapter 9

THE CROSS CHANGED EVERYTHING

As we shift from an Old Covenant perspective on worship to that of the New, we find ourselves working from a different language base as far as bible translation goes. Because of this change, we are going to take a moment to update our worship definitions.

New Testament Definitions

In the New Testament, there are two words rendered as "worship." They are translated out of the Greek language as follows:

Worship – "Proskuneo" To bring a sacrifice, bow down, pay homage, and worship. There are other variations of this word, one of them being to "kiss." It means virtually the same thing as its Hebrew counterpart "Shachah."

Worship – "Latreuo" This word implies that our lifestyle and service to the Lord is the act of worship. It shadows the Hebrew word "Avodah."

The two sided "worship coin" mirrors perfectly in both the Old and the New Testament. In the first case, worship is something we set out to do in a personal or corporate gathering, whereas in the second, it is a 24/7 rendering of our lives as a sacrifice. These two thoughts, once again, dovetail together to bring a full understanding of worship.

The House of Worship

In our journey through the bible, we have been building a house of worship. We started by setting a cornerstone in place. Sacrifice is the foundation that worship rests on. Without it, there is nothing to bring, nothing to burn. We then put up the walls of the house. The walls were built out of glory. God's glory surrounds our sacrifices of worship and the consuming fire of God burns what is laid on the altar.

We then talked about God's presence. The presence covers worship with a blanket of love and light. It is the roof of our house. After putting on the roof, we met the Levites—the workers of the house—called from birth to care for all things related to the worship of God's people. After that, we put a key piece of furniture in the house, the ark. We also built some rooms like the holy place where the ark was kept.

In this chapter, we are going to talk about the cross. The house of worship was altered significantly in the shadow of the cross. Even though the foundation, the walls, and the roof remained intact, the house was put into a state of renovations and given a complete update by Jesus.

There is quite a difference between the worship of the Old Covenant and that of the New. Once Jesus came, went to the cross, and was resurrected, worship changed—so much so that hardly a trace remains of the previous 4000 years of worship history.

In our modern world, it is hard for us to even imagine the process of killing animals, sprinkling blood, and burning things on an altar as worship. Today, we go to a gathering, sing some songs, and refer to it as worship. Thankfully, everything we experience now is because of the cross.

A Cross Encounter

A few years ago, I had an encounter with the cross that forever changed me. It began as a dream. I was on an island. There were slaves all around me, and oppression as far as I could see. I was thinking about running to safety when I realized that I was also a slave. Before I could make a move, a cruel master came up and started beating and threatening me. Each island slave had a job—mine was to dig in the dirt with my bare hands. I began scraping away at the hard soil with my fingers until they were bleeding and raw.

> *God's presence covers worship with a blanket of light and love*

As I clawed the ground, the island began to fade, and I found myself bound by chains next to a Roman whipping post. I have seen the "Passion of the Christ" movie several times but this was no movie. There were no actors, no props, and there was no soundtrack. This was absolutely real.

A multi-dimensional scene began to develop in front of my eyes. The soldiers came to get me, dragging me toward the post, but as they did, I saw another person out of the corner of my eye. He put out his hand in a "stop" motion and the soldiers relented, throwing me to the ground. They grabbed him and took him to the post instead. I then recognized the stranger as Jesus. I watched as they literally took Him apart with their whips. It was the most beyond-cruel thing I had ever seen in my life.

As this scene faded away, another one began to materialize and I realized that I was on the summit of a hill. There were soldiers everywhere and a wooden cross lying on the ground. The soldiers grabbed me and started shoving me toward the cross. I was the one who deserved to die. They took my hand and put it on the wood. I could feel the splinters on the back of my hand but when I looked over, there was

> *The bloodstained spectacle of the cross was the ultimate expression of worship for all time*

Jesus. Different things stand out in a moment like this, but what caught my eye was how big His nose was. He looked at me and put out His hand instead. They didn't take it—He gave it.

Then I saw the nails. They were six inches long, thick at the top, and shaped down to a point at the bottom. Jesus was looking straight into my eyes when the hammer went down—then the other hand, then the feet. It would always nearly happen to me. Then He would offer himself. The feet seemed to be the most painful and I knew that He was purchasing my Shalom—my peace. At that point I saw that He was doing everything by sheer faith.

When they lifted the cross up, I saw His separation from the Father. It seemed to rend the heart of God. Then I witnessed something that I don't know if I will ever be able to fully put into words. I saw fire and glory. It engulfed Jesus in what appeared to be a spontaneous combustion. At this moment, I realized that the cross was one grand act of worship. I also had a living revelation of the verse, *"There is no greater love than to lay down one's life for one's friends."*

When I woke up, my heart was so overcome with a sense of helplessness, gratitude, and the fear of God that it took me several hours to recover. I will never forget the love with which Jesus looked at me, and the fire. This was one of the most life shaping encounters that I have ever had. It has deeply affected my view of worship and my outlook on life.

Selah – pause in His presence

The Ultimate Sacrifice

I would like to say with much reverence, that the blood-stained spectacle of the cross was the ultimate expression of worship for all time. It was so complete that it paved the way for us to have a whole new relationship with God, and it forever realigned the way that we worship. Jesus' offering of worship was the blood sacrifice to end all blood sacrifices.

Here are a few verses that speak about the worship offered on the cross.

> *Jesus carried his own cross out of the city to the place called "The Skull," which in Aramaic is Golgotha.*

> (John 19:17 TPT)

In remembering the sacrifice of Abraham and Isaac, the wood was laid on Isaac. In this scripture we see Jesus also carrying the wood—the cross, to His own sacrifice.

> *If animal sacrifices could once and for all eliminate sin, they would have ceased to be offered and the worshipers would have clean consciences. Instead, once was not enough so by the repetitive sacrifices year after year, the worshipers were continually reminded of their sins, with their hearts still impure. For what power does the blood of bulls and goats have to remove sin's guilt?*
>
> *So when Jesus the Messiah came into the world he said, "Since your ultimate desire was not another animal sacrifice, you have clothed me with a body that I might offer myself instead! Multiple burnt offerings and sin-offerings cannot satisfy your justice. So I said to you, 'God—I will be the One to go and do your will, to fulfill all that is written of me in your Word!'"*

(Hebrews 10:3-7 TPT)

This passage shows how the Old Testament sacrifices of worship only temporarily covered sin. God never wanted those blood sacrifices, but they were a necessity in the age of law. When Jesus came to our earth, He was given a body, one prepared and fit for a final sacrifice. Upon going to the cross, He satisfied the demand of the law, and in the ultimate act of worship, made us holy through the offering of His body once and for all!

In view of the cross, these next verses use classic worship terminology such as "offered," "sacrifice," and "pleasing aroma."

Live a life filled with love, following the example of Christ. He loved us and offered himself as a sacrifice for us, a pleasing aroma to God.

(Ephesians 5:2)

The Glory of the Cross

These next words were spoken by Jesus just hours before He and the disciples headed to the garden of Gethsemane:

Lifting up His eyes to heaven, He said, "Father, the hour has come; glorify Your Son, that the Son may glorify You."

(John 17:1 NASB)

There is one essential element needed to complete a sacrifice of worship—fire to consume the offering. For this reason, on the evening before going to the cross, Jesus petitioned the Father to glorify Him. In this prayer, Jesus was asking the Father to turn Him into a fiery burning standard on that cross! In the final act of blood sacrifice, Jesus was intent on His body going up in a burning display of flames and glory, an unforgettable example of all-consuming fire and worship for the whole world to see.

> *The realization that glory burns up sacrifice gives the phrase, "The glory of the cross," a whole new meaning*

By the time Jesus died, He was marred more than any other man, disfigured beyond comprehension. He was no more recognizable than a pile of smoldering ashes. The realization that glory burns up sacrifice gives the phrase, "The glory of the cross," a whole new meaning.

Jesus' worship on the cross was the grandest sacrifice of worship ever offered, and He did it all by faith. What a hero we have in our Savior. Words cannot begin to describe His matchless beauty!

Selah – pause in His Presence

The Torn Veil

Once Jesus cried out the words, *"It is finished!"* His earthly mission was complete. At that moment, the veil of the temple, separating the holy of holies from the rest of the world, was torn from top to bottom.

The veil was legendary. It was a shroud of interwoven cloth that Jewish tradition tells us was the thickness of a man's hand. It was also thirty feet high. The force required to rend it would have been significant.

> *In the time in which we live after the cross, the ark looks very human—we are the ark*

The holy of holies with its thick veil was a necessity in the law-based worship system. It came about when God's people decided that they didn't want to know Him directly in the wilderness. Once the veil was torn, the presence of God that used to reside upon the ark was set free.

I have always imagined this event similar to a caged room full of restrained and pent-up doves. Think of the walls of their enclosure being torn down in one sweeping motion. Picture the commotion as a whole flock of pure white birds realize they are finally free—scattering across the sky in a flurry of excitement and abandon.

The liberation of God's presence from the holy of holies forever changed how we worship.

The New and Improved Ark!

The torn veil didn't actually reveal the ark. It had been missing for centuries already, hidden away when God's people went into captivity. So the question remains—is there an ark in the New Covenant? If we are going to worship in the presence of the glory, we will need to find it once again.

In the time in which we live after the cross, there is no longer one ark. There are millions, possibly even billions of them and they look very human. We are the ark!

The glory of God that escaped from behind the torn veil now finds its home in vessels made out of clay.

> *For God, who said, "Let brilliant light shine out of darkness," is the one who has cascaded his light into us—the brilliant dawning light of the glorious knowledge of God as we gaze into the face of Jesus Christ. We are like common clay jars that carry this glorious treasure within.*

(2 Corinthians 4:6-7 TPT)

Because each one of us has been made a priest before God, the presence that rested on the shoulders of the priests now rests in and upon us. In proportion, we as humans are even about the same size as the ark.

The items that were once inside the ark—the stone tablets containing the Ten Commandments, a jar of manna, and a branch that constantly budded with life, now live inside of us in the form of grace. The stone has been done away with. It has been replaced with a soft, new heart with a new commandment written on it—the law of love.

I will remove from them their heart of stone and give them a heart of flesh.

(Ezekiel 11:19)

I will put my law in their minds and write it on their hearts.

(Jeremiah 31:33)

For the entire law is fulfilled in keeping this one command: "Love your neighbor as yourself."

(Galatians 5:14)

In Christ, we also have a never-ending supply of daily bread, as well as a source of life that makes us into trees, bearing fruit all year round.

Return to the Ark-tent

It is no secret that by the time Jesus came to the earth, worship needed a complete overhaul. It had taken on many different shapes and suffered much abuse down through the centuries. After the garden of Eden, it existed in the form of burnt offerings. Once the Law of Moses was established, it came under the jurisdiction of the tabernacle system. When David moved the ark into the ark-tent (the tabernacle of David), worship became a very intimate act directly in front of the ark. Once Solomon built his new temple, it reverted back to a law-based model again. This system

> *The cross raised up the tabernacle of David again—the humble ark tent*

eventually became corrupt, disintegrating into a religious order that killed its own Savior.

So where did God choose to land with worship once the work of the cross was complete? Why do we get to sing songs instead of sacrificing animals? Why can we gather and worship directly and freely?

> *"After these things I will return to you and raise up the tabernacle of David that has fallen into ruin. I will restore and rebuild what David experienced so that all of humanity will be able to encounter the Lord including the gentiles whom I have called to be my very own," says the Lord.*

(Acts 15:15-17 TPT)

Speaking of the time frame after the cross, this passage confirms that God chose to bring worship back to a place mirroring the few short years when He was face to face with His Levite worshipers. The cross raised up the tabernacle of David again—the humble ark-tent. It rebuilt what David experienced. Because of a return back to intimate worship, all of humanity is now able to encounter the Lord.

Why do we get to experience worship so freely—because of the cross.

Why do we get to sing and play instruments as we worship—because of the cross.

Why do we get to express worship in different art forms such as dancing, painting, and writing—because of the cross.

Why can we be encountered with glory and presence as we worship—because of the cross!

This is our time! We are worshiping in David's tabernacle once again! What a unique and beautiful grace we have been given.

Renovations Complete

What does the house of worship look like in the shadow of the cross? The cornerstone is still sacrifice—providing a sure and solid foundation for any worship experience. Every act of worship, even an intimate one, is a sacrifice.

The walls are still made of glory. God's glory is still the only fire worthy of consuming our sacrifices of worship. The presence still descends on the worship of God's people, providing the roof of our house.

However, the front wall of the house has been completely removed. All that remains is an open concept porch with a wide-open door. Instead of a single piece of furniture containing God's presence hidden behind a veil, the nations now enter freely. Each person now carries the presence in and out of the house, coming directly before the Lord in worship. The house is now a place of celebration. In it is heard the sound of singing and dancing. It also has a brand-new color scheme—the look of God's artists as they create, filling the walls with images of freedom and grace.

There are no more blood sacrifices, no more hoops to jump through, and no more rules to follow in order to make suitable sacrifices according to law. Now and forevermore, it is just God's people and His presence.

Thank you, Jesus, for the complete, finished work of the cross! Eternity will not be long enough to tell of it!

ENCOUNTERED *in* WORSHIP

Chapter 10

WORSHIP IN SPIRIT

As we set foot on the veranda of our newly renovated house of worship, we are going to look at what Jesus had to say about worship.

While on a journey through Samaria, Jesus had an encounter with a Samaritan woman beside a well. The conversation between them was somewhat awkward at first, but Jesus soon found a way to speak words of life to her. The woman sensed that He was a prophet and asked a bold question—one that seemed to have been bothering her for some time. She had been wondering where they should worship.

The Samaritan people worshiped on a mountain in Samaria, while the Jews worshiped in Jerusalem at the temple. The physical location of worship had become a point of contention between the two cultures, with the Jews always holding superiority over the Samaritans. Jesus' response not only answered the woman's question, it also set a new standard for worship.

Jesus replied, "Believe me, dear woman, the time is coming when it will no longer matter whether you worship the Father on this mountain or in Jerusalem. But the time is coming—indeed it's here now—when true worshipers will worship the Father in spirit and in truth. The Father is looking for those who will worship him that way. For God is Spirit, so those who worship him must worship in spirit and in truth."

(John 4:21, 23-24)

There is a lot to discover in these phrases spoken by Jesus. His answer first announced a new location for worship—something unprecedented because God's people were only allowed to worship in a few specified places. The new site was

Seeing has always been an important part of the worship experience

not on a Samaritan mountain or in Jerusalem anymore, it was somewhere called "in spirit."

The next part of Jesus' answer revealed a heart attitude that goes along with the new location. Worship must be done "in truth." Truth is experienced when nothing is hidden.

Jesus also gave us a secret to turning the Father's face. Evidently God is searching the earth for "in spirit and truth" worshipers. If we would like to catch His eye, it is clear what we need to be doing.

Where Was That Again?

The question remains, where is "in spirit," and how can we go there to worship? A quick word search reveals that this new location is no longer geographical. It is a place found in the breath and atmosphere of heaven. The Greek phrase translated "in spirit" consists of two words: "en" (in), and "pheuma" (breath or spirit). It is a kingdom phrase.

Imagine, for a moment, that you are on a quest to bring an offering of worship before a king. In order to worship him, you will need to find his kingdom. Then you will have to go to the palace where he lives, bow down before him, and present your offering.

In speaking of the king of the universe, where is our Father God? He exists in the spirit realm—in the kingdom of heaven! *"Our Father, who is in heaven, hallowed be Your name."* If we want to worship Him, we will have to go there. Here is how Jesus described God's kingdom:

> *"The Kingdom of God does not come in such a way as to be seen. No one will say, 'Look, here it is!' or, 'There it is!'; because the Kingdom of God is **within** you."*

(Luke 17:21 GNT)

The word "within" in this verse is the Greek word "entos." It means "inside." The kingdom of God is inside you. In order to worship in a New Covenant way, we are going to have to go to the kingdom of God which is inside us, find God, and worship Him there.

In my travels and experiences, I find few people who know this inner sanctuary even exists. Worship has always required faith, and to find this inner kingdom requires faith. It also requires the ability to see. Seeing has always been an important part of the worship experience.

For this reason, I believe that God has given each one of us the ability to see into the spirit realm. He has also given the same gift to groups of people gathered in Jesus' name. We have been made with an inner portal to the place where God is, specifically, heaven.

Right from the beginning, our human spirit was created to interface with heaven. This is not just a place that we go when we die. If you consider that, *"We have died and our lives are hidden with Christ,"* we can go to heaven every day of our lives! In fact, we must enter the atmosphere and breath of heaven in order to worship "in spirit."

John's Encounter

Here is another example of "in spirit" worship. John was exiled on a small island because of his faith when he had an awe-inspiring encounter.

> *It was the Lord's Day, and I was worshiping in the Spirit. Suddenly, I heard behind me a loud voice like a trumpet blast.*

(Revelation 1:10)

When John turned to see where the voice was coming from, his eyes were opened to the heavenly realm. Jesus was standing in front of him and gave him a series of messages for the church scattered across Asia. After the messages were written down, the encounter continued with phase two.

> *Then as I looked, I saw a door standing open in heaven, and the same voice I had heard before spoke to me like a trumpet*

blast. The voice said, "Come up here, and I will show you what must happen after this." And instantly I was in the Spirit, and I saw a throne in heaven and someone sitting on it.

(Revelation 4:1-2)

The first thing John did was to look. With his inner eyes focused on the seeing realm, John saw an open door in heaven. A voice then spoke to him, giving him an invitation, "Come up here." Immediately John was in the Spirit. The phrase used in both of John's encounters, "in the Spirit," is the same Greek phrase that Jesus spoke to the woman at the well, "en pheuma," (in breath or spirit).

Seeing? Me? Really?

My own journey into the seeing realm didn't come easy to me. I came from a place where "seeing" was considered dangerous and the product of an over active imagination. As I began to search for deeper worship in my life, the Holy Spirit began to speak to me about the eyes of my heart. He told me that I was

> *We must enter the atmosphere and breath of heaven in order to worship in spirit*

blind and that I needed eye salve. I wasn't sure what this meant, but I found a reference to it at the end of the third chapter of Revelation, part of John's message to the church of Laodicea—a church that couldn't see.

One day the Holy Spirit told me that if I wanted to connect with the atmosphere of heaven on a consistent basis, I should read the fourth chapter of Revelation every day. As I did so, impressions of heaven started taking hold of my heart.

Still, my longing was for more than just to read about the kingdom of heaven. I started to cry out for my eyes to be anointed with spiritual eye salve and for my ears to be sensitized to the sound of Jesus knocking on the door of my heart (also found in John's letter to Laodicea). I began to change my thinking when it came to preconceived ideas of what I could or couldn't see. I wanted to be a person who could worship with full sight rather than blindly—I wanted to be able to worship in spirit and in truth.

In the weeks that followed, a few times in my night dreams I heard the sound of someone knocking on a door. I didn't even know where the door was but I decided to search for it. I began to sit for hours in the presence of God. I would worship and wait, hoping to find the place in my heart that opened up to the kingdom of heaven that I knew was inside me.

One day, while I was waiting on the Lord, I saw an unpretentious wooden door in front of me. This was a definite breakthrough! The problem was I couldn't find the door handle. A few days later I saw the same door again but this time I noticed a keyhole in it. I somehow managed to kneel down and peer through the keyhole. I could see a light on the other side brighter than anything I had ever seen on earth.

The next week, I saw the same door and keyhole, and this time I found a key on the ground. I was able to put the key into the keyhole and unlock the door but I still couldn't get the door open. The next day, I succeeded in opening the door just a crack. I saw light flooding through the crack like I had never seen before. Eventually I learned to open the door.

At first I had to let my spiritual eyes adjust to the light and I could only go a few steps inside. Over a period of weeks, I ventured further and further. This whole process took persistence and patience. I had to go slowly. Although I am now familiar with the "seeing" realm, at that time I hardly knew it existed and it had to be awakened in me in baby steps.

After I got used to this environment, I began to explore the new world I had discovered. At this point in time, some very convincing things started to happen. I would often wonder if what I was perceiving was real or not. However, I would see something in the spirit world and later that day experience the same thing in the natural world. It was as if the Holy Spirit was drawing me forward step by step into this encounter—calling me up, inviting me to press in and not give up.

I also began to realize that each time I entered into heavenly places, the glory of God would rest on me for the remainder of the day. I began to have such a hunger to enter the kingdom that I could think of little else. The further I ventured the clearer the picture became. Through much diligence and perseverance, I discovered rivers, houses, pathways, and a garden.

It was here that I met Jesus for the first time. One day, standing by a fountain, I noticed someone beside me who was holding a crystal goblet. He dipped it in the water and then offered me a drink. At first all I could see was His hand, but if you've ever seen the hands of Jesus, there is no mistaking them because of the nail holes.

I sat on a nearby bench and learned to talk with Him. My conversations with Jesus were not necessarily profound, but I realized that He was interested in the details of my life, even small things. He asked me questions like, "How was your day?" or "How did your meeting go this morning?"

One thing I learned quickly was that if I would come to Him without any agenda, He would answer every question that was on my mind without me even asking. On the other hand, if I came with a mind full of questions, things could get rather awkward.

I also realized that Jesus loves to talk about the Father. One day, He asked me if I would like to go for a walk. He took me on a lengthy journey that eventually led me to the throne. It was here that I learned to bring my worship directly before the Father of Creation.

Selah – pause in His Presence

Thanks, Praise, Worship

In my quest to worship "in spirit," I have discovered that there is a pathway that leads to the heart of God and to the

> *God is a being of creativity, spontaneity, and diversity*

seeing realm. It is found in the process of giving thanks, bringing a sacrifice of praise, and offering up worship. Although I have been down this road many times in both personal and corporate worship settings, I am quick to say that worship defies a formula. It is part of the communication process between heaven and earth—a relationship in which no two encounters are the same.

We as humans love things that are predictable. God on the other hand is a being of creativity, spontaneity, and diversity.

Examples from the Psalms

Psalm 95 starts with an exhortation to sing to the Lord. We are encouraged to come before His presence with thanksgiving. The Psalm moves into various forms of praise including shouting joyfully, and telling about the works and nature of God. Then we see a change in the atmosphere, *"Come let us worship and bow down, let us kneel before the Lord our Maker."*

Psalm 96 is much the same. It starts with singing, telling of the deeds of God, and thanksgiving. It transitions into praise—proclaiming the nature of God and His greatness. The psalmist ascribes, or gives to the Lord the glory and strength that is due His name. We then see a shift, *"Bring an offering and come into His courts. Worship the Lord in the splendor of holiness."*

A Pathway to the Throne

There are many times when I come to commune with God, that I feel little in the way of His presence resting upon me. I am prone to bad days and low times just like everyone else. For this reason, I like to view worship as a journey.

> *Enter his gates with thanksgiving and his courts with praise; give thanks to him and praise his name.*

> (Psalm 100:4 NIV)

I have learned to start by giving thanks to the Lord. Both thanksgiving and praise act as gateways to God's presence. For the first while, I might sense nothing, but if I focus my mind on all He has done, my soul will eventually start to rejoice in Him. I have found that rejoicing is a powerful way to open up the heavens, and a highly effective spiritual weapon.

You will call your walls salvation, and your gates praise.

(Isaiah 60:18 NASB)

Next I will offer up a sacrifice of praise to His name, declaring who God is and recounting His greatness. If I persist long enough, the Holy Spirit will always lead me forward toward the glory. As I express my affections to Him, I start to feel His presence warming my heart.

The only things that can stop the manifestation of God's presence are distractions, impatience, and agenda. Shame and guilt will also stop the progression of worship but not because God is holding out on us. God did not withdraw His presence from Adam and Eve when they sinned—He actually went looking for them. They were the ones who chose to hide. I have determined that no matter what I have done, I will run with every ounce of strength that I have directly toward God's presence.

Praise Opens the Door

Once Jesus begins to inhabit my praises the atmosphere will start to change. His glorious face turns in my direction and an upward call is given. A gate is opened and a window of opportunity arises to enter into a holy, heavenly environment. It is a doorway to "in spirit" worship. As the heavens open up and the angels begin to interact with the worship, the glory of God starts to fill the place of worship. The journey now takes on a whole new dimension of depth and presence.

We can give a sacrifice of thanksgiving when it seems there is nothing to be thankful for. We can bring an offering of praise when God's goodness is the only praiseworthy thing in our lives. But in worship, we become the offering. It is our very lives, everything we are and ever hope to be, and all of our dreams that we surrender in adoration before the throne. At this point in time, in my own worship encounters, the presence of God starts to burn in and around me.

In the middle of everything, I always leave deliberate space for God to move on my heart. Far too often, worship gets confined to a one-way conversation. We talk at, or sing at God with closed ears. Yet some of the most life shaping downloads and words I have experienced *In worship, we become the offering* have been in worship. When we focus our eyes on Jesus, when His presence envelops us, we instinctively find ourselves in a perfect posture for receiving.

In this setting, healing is often released. In my life experience, worship has been a faithful healing balm—physically, emotionally, and spiritually. I have also seen healing manifested in corporate worship settings. One time, a person with some broken bones from an automobile accident was healed just a few rows in front of me as we simply worshiped.

There is an ancient word that I have used numerous times in this book: "Selah." It means, "pause in His presence." In worship, we need to learn how to stop, listen for God's voice, and wait.

Glory Surfing

Often, in this holy place, God's glory will begin to roll in like the waves of the ocean. There will be more worship, then another wave of glory to consume the worship. This cycle can go on for hours on end.

There are times when I am caught up in the presence and I lose track of where I am here on this earth. There are other times when I am very much on earth—my eyes simply focused on Jesus with His glory calling me up higher.

I have also been in many corporate worship services where entire groups of worshipers have purposed to fix their eyes on Jesus. In His presence, a door opens to the heavens and the call to "come up here" sounds out to those who will listen. On these occasions, the glory that interacts with God's people is beyond description. Entire congregations can be transported into heavenly places! I live for these times. Without them, life holds very little meaning for me.

> *The incredible call, "come up here," is offered without reservation to each and every person who believes in Jesus*

I believe that the incredible call "come up here," is offered without reservation to each and every person who believes in Jesus. It is an open, 24/7 invitation to a place called "in spirit."

Selah – pause in His presence

A profound change has taken place in me as I have pressed in to worship in this way. If you ask me for specific "hows," it is actually very simple. I have learned to quiet my heart in the presence of the Lord, let this earth fade away, and enter into another realm. Is it literal or mystical? I am not sure, possibly both.

In whatever directions the Holy Spirit chooses to lead, we are wise to never limit God or set boundaries on what He can and can't do. To do so is only to rob ourselves of the two-way conversation, the call and the response, the offering and the glory, and the transformation that happens as we worship.

ENCOUNTERED *in* WORSHIP

Chapter 11

WORSHIP IN TRUTH

We are going to throw open all of the windows of our worship house. Old Testament worshipers used to go through an exacting practice of cleansing and preparation. I am thankful that through the cross, Jesus has placed us into a new setting with only one requirement—truth. This new posture of worship is found in vulnerability.

> *Claiming to be wise, they became fools, and exchanged the glory of the immortal God for images resembling mortal man and birds and animals and creeping things. Therefore, God gave them up in the lusts of their hearts to impurity, to the dishonoring of their bodies among themselves, because they exchanged the truth about God for a lie and worshiped and served the creature rather than the Creator, who is blessed forever!*

> (Romans 1:22-25 ESV)

The Worship Exchange

In the before-mentioned passage, Paul is talking about idol worship but he brings out a profound thought—he highlights something that happens when we worship in truth. In the process of worship, there is an exchange that takes place. We are trading glory with the object of our worship.

In the case of true God worship, we surrender all of the glory on our lives to Him. In return, He shines the countenance of His face back on us, filling us with even more glory than we could ever imagine. In my estimation, this is a pretty sweet deal.

By contrast, when worshiping outside of truth (idol worship), the exchange is quite frightful. These individuals give the glory on their lives to an idol, worshiping an image with a demonic presence behind it. As a result, they become corrupted with an inferior glory, bringing about impurity and a body that trends toward evil.

Truth

Truth – *To be in a state of not concealing anything—authenticity, accuracy, faith, revelation, sincerity, and integrity.*

Worshiping "in truth" is revealed when we offer all. There is no other acceptable sacrifice but one given out of pure honesty. God knows if we are holding anything back from Him. There is no way of deceiving such a remarkable being as our Father in heaven. He desires "truth" in the innermost being. (Psalm 51:6)

The Lord is close to all who call on him, yes, to all who call on him in truth.

(Psalm 145:18)

An Encounter with Heaven

The bible describes the New Jerusalem as a cube—1500 miles in length, width, and height. In my experiences, it seems as if there are multiple layers and massive lifts that transport you from one level to the next. Heaven's vastness makes you feel like you are only seeing one billionth of what is there. Although I have been there many times, one night, a few

> *Worship "in truth" is revealed when we offer all*

years ago, I was given a special grace. Since the encounter I am about to describe, I have never been the same and my view of worship has changed markedly.

When I went to bed that night, my mind was pondering end time events. As I drifted off to sleep, I began to dream, but the dream transported me to a different world, as often happens. When I became aware of my surroundings, I discovered that I was right near the center of heaven, in the area of the throne.

What unfolded next was a scene as is described in the fourth chapter of the book of Revelation. Everything was extremely bright and loud, and worship seemed to engulf me from every angle. There were millions of angels as well as an uncountable number of redeemed ones singing, dancing, and praising. Many things happened that I simply could not retain or bring back as memories, but a few images stood out to me.

The first persons I noticed were the twenty-four elders. I was very close to them; I saw them from the ground level. Their entire focus was intent on one thing alone—worship. They had beautiful crowns in their hands that they would throw toward the throne. These crowns would have been worth millions of dollars here on earth, representing great honor.

However, it almost seemed like the crowns were on invisible rubber bands. It didn't matter how hard they were thrown, they would always come back into their hands. These actions gave me a new understanding of the word "cast." From what I could see, the elders were desperately trying to get rid of their crowns.

Then I noticed Father God. As I gazed at Him, I realized that in heaven, facial expressions and non-verbal cues account for the majority of all communication. He would say things with just one facial expression that seemed to speak a trillion words. His face was so uniquely expressive that He didn't even need to use words.

In that moment, I gained a whole new understanding of what it means to worship in truth. There is nothing hidden in heaven. On earth our thoughts are concealed from others, but in heaven, each thought is broadcast for everyone to know. Everything is open and vulnerable. Surprisingly, there was a great sense of freedom and relief for me in knowing that I couldn't hide anything. I grasped the meaning of the phrase, "You will know the truth, and the truth will set you free." (John 8:32)

The next thing that caught my attention were four very strange looking living beings. They were standing, one at each corner of the throne. They were full of eyes and I knew they saw everything. I almost laughed because they had an odd characteristic that I didn't expect. Have you ever seen a teenager who has just had a growth spurt and their coordination hasn't yet caught up with their limbs? That was the impression I got from these creatures. They were tall, lanky, slightly awkward, and they seemed to have grown too fast.

The four creatures faced the throne and were constantly watching God's every move. They were very demonstrative, using their hands and waving them, not overhead, but underhanded toward the throne. They were saying "Holy, holy, holy," over and over again. I was struck by how serious they were about their worship. Nothing escaped their attention.

Whenever God would change His position slightly, it was as if they saw a whole new side of Him, and they would begin worshiping all over again. Somehow, I knew this had been going on for eternities past and that the wonders of God were simply inexhaustible. It also gave me a whole new understanding of the word "shift," a term that we use so freely and carelessly in our church circles. All God has done is to shift on his throne. Imagine what would happen if He ever decided to stand up! Their worship was filled with wonder, humor, and fear, but they were also feisty and bold. They had a great respect for, and a great rapport with God all at the same time.

Then, in a moment, the magnitude of worship in heaven and on earth unfolded and came crashing down on me in a way that I can't even describe. I was aware that we are caught up in a grand irony of heaven, something so much bigger than any of us know. I realized that worship has been going on for eternity upon eternity.

I also saw that we, here on earth, have little idea of what is happening when we worship. We think our worship stands on its own, but it is all part of a massive universal cycle that is constantly returning glory to God. If there is such a thing as a "spirit of worship," then worship is a living entity, rather than something that we do.

As I surveyed the vastness of the scene in front of me and tried to grapple with a mountain's worth of emotions and thoughts, the Father turned His face toward me and caught my eye. He gave me a look that spoke a billion words. In essence, the look said, "You think you have it all figured out, don't you," but He said it with an expression of love, humor,

> *I have learned that the Father loves to reveal heaven to us*

and grace that touched my heart to the core. I was humbled to realize how limited my understanding was. When I woke, I was so undone by the experience that I began sobbing uncontrollably. Glory pain was pulsing through my spirit and soul, and I had no strength.

Selah – pause in His presence

I used to be reluctant to tell of my experiences in heaven but I have realized that there is a part of each of us that longs for eternity. I am not sharing my encounters because I am special in any way. In fact, I am a most unlikely seeing realm candidate. I have many friends whose inner eyes see into heavenly places so naturally that it makes what I do seem archaic and awkward. I encourage anyone who might be in a place of self-doubt over your qualifications for this journey—don't give up. At one time, I didn't think it was possible for me either.

Is it necessary to have an all-out encounter with heaven each time we worship? No. On the other hand, don't assume that Jesus doesn't want to pull you closer than you have ever imagined.

I have learned that the Father loves to reveal heaven to us. He pursues us, drawing us into places of bliss and wonder in His presence.

Let's See

I would like to invite you to open the eyes of your heart. Take a moment to focus. Close your eyes and picture the throne of God. Now, using your earthly eyes only as receptacles for what is on the page, read these next paragraphs slowly, phrase by phrase—with your inner eyes. Don't allow a sentence to go by without letting it bring an image to your heart.

Then as I looked, I saw a door standing open in heaven, and the same voice I had heard before spoke to me like a trumpet blast. The voice said, "Come up here, and I will show you what must happen after this." And instantly I was in the Spirit, and I saw a throne in heaven and someone sitting on it. The one sitting on the throne was as brilliant as gemstones—like jasper and carnelian. And the glow of an emerald circled his throne like a rainbow.

Twenty-four thrones surrounded him, and twenty-four elders sat on them. They were all clothed in white and had gold crowns on their heads. From the throne came flashes of lightning and the rumble of thunder. And in front of the throne were seven torches with burning flames. This is the sevenfold Spirit of God. In front of the throne was a shiny sea of glass, sparkling like crystal.

In the center and around the throne were four living beings, each covered with eyes, front and back. The first of these living beings was like a lion; the second was like an ox; the third had a human face; and the fourth was like an eagle in flight. Each of these living beings had six wings, and their wings were covered all over with eyes, inside and out. Day after day and night after night they keep on saying, "Holy, holy, holy is the Lord God, the Almighty—the one who always was, who is, and who is still to come."

Whenever the living beings give glory and honor and thanks to the one sitting on the throne (the one who lives forever and ever), the twenty-four elders fall down and worship the one sitting on the throne (the one who lives forever and ever). And they lay their crowns before the throne and say, "You are worthy, O Lord our God, to receive glory and honor and power. For you created all things, and they exist because you created what you pleased."

Revelation 4

Selah – pause in His presence

Let's Worship

Since at this moment we are all "in spirit," we are going to spend some time worshiping together. Worship doesn't require us to be perfect. It only requires that we are focused on heaven and that we are honest—in spirit and in truth.

Because we are going before the king, let's take a minute to think of what is in our hands. In the case of the elders, it is their crowns. Let's ask the Holy Spirit what He is asking *us* to lay down before the throne. What glory has been given to us, what honor have we been blessed with, what giftings, power, strength? Are there any

> *Worship only requires that we are focused on heaven and that we are honest*

dreams, relationships, questions, failures, or victories? Are we afraid of something, have we been misunderstood, have we created something for which we have been complimented? How about our lives, our bodies, our hearts, our souls?

The "in truth" part of worship is contained in the fact that there is no deceiving our Father in heaven—so let's be absolutely honest with Him. There is no place more secure than the altar of worship. Every sacrifice of worship is divinely protected. If He asks for something, let's determine to bring it all and offer it with our whole hearts. He is worthy of it all.

Now let's picture ourselves with the elders. They are very human people in heaven, full of love and acceptance. We are safe with them—they understand everything that we are going through because they once lived on earth just like we do.

We are not alone in our worship. The entire universe is doing the same thing that we are getting ready to do right now—returning all glory back to the place where it came from, to the Father of all creation.

At this point in time, the presence of heaven is surrounding us as we kneel, bowing before the feet of the Father. Now,

"In truth" worship is an expression of the heart

together with the elders, let's put our eyes on the worthy One and cast what is in our hands before the throne—let go of it completely. Allow the fire of God's glory to consume it. Watch it burn.

Selah – pause in His presence

Now let's look up at the One on the throne again.

Wait! His head is turning our way. Could it be? Yes! He is looking straight at each one of us and He is smiling—His countenance is beaming with glory!

He is saying something—what is it? Be still, listen …

What used to be an agitating question doesn't seem to matter anymore. With all dreams surrendered, He is downloading new ideas now, bringing clarity and even better plans. His glory is covering us, replenishing us with new vigor and fresh power. The broken bodies that we laid down before Him are being healed in His presence—strength is being renewed, hearts are being restored. Things from the past are dropping off effortlessly as we gaze into His face. We are being changed into His image.

Is there something else that He is worthy of? Is anybody ready for round two? Why not go from glory to glory, like surfers catching the swells of His presence, bringing all that we have and are before Him time and time again. Let's empty ourselves out completely, holding nothing back in humble adoration, praise, and thankfulness—worshiping "in spirit" and "in truth."

Selah – pause in His presence

A Heart Expression

"In truth" worship is an expression of the heart. It requires our lives to be fully surrendered—it is spiritual open-heart surgery. Worship, by nature, can be done with nothing less than our entire heart, soul, mind, and strength. It requires "engaging" in a conversation, an expression, and an offering. It requires the opening up of emotions, vulnerability, and sacrifice.

Making a sacrifice is sometimes painful. There is a phrase that I use to describe this pain—it hurts so good! I often have people ask me what it is like to spend time in heavenly environments saturated with God's glory. In response, I say that the glory of God is both the most exhilarating and the most painful place you could ever be in at the same time. Glory consumes in a most wonderful way. The pain that it brings deep down in the core of your being is extremely healing in the same breath. It is life changing and revolutionary.

> *Since we are receiving our rights to an unshakeable kingdom, we should be extremely thankful and offer God the purest worship that delights his heart as we lay down our lives in absolute surrender, filled with awe. For our God is a holy, devouring fire!*

(Hebrews 12:28-29 TPT)

Fire burns. When we feel our heart burning during worship, we can be assured that the fire is being stoked and our lives are on the altar.

I am convinced that a life given as a sacrifice in the presence of God's glory embodies the true meaning of the phrase, "You must lose your life to find it."

Kingdom Worship

Returning to the book of Revelation, here is a follow-up to the heavenly scene we have been taking in.

> *And the four living beings and the twenty-four elders fell down before the Lamb. Each one had a harp, and they held gold bowls filled with incense, which are the prayers of God's people.*

(Revelation 5:8)

The word translated "prayers" here is the Greek word "proseuche." It means prayers, supplications, and worship!

Worship is an awe-inspiring kingdom activity. Whether we realize it or not, there are millions, possibly billions of angels, redeemed ones, and other glorified beings worshiping God at this moment. The cherubim are crying "holy," and the elders are falling down and casting their crowns. The breathtaking part is that we, here on earth, are invited to join in, adding a planetary vibe to the great celebration of worship that is constantly in progress.

> *Our God is constantly smelling the soothing aroma of our worship*

Bowls of Incense

Have you ever wondered what worship, offered here on earth, looks like in heaven? Both the four creatures and the elders hold something in their hands—bowls containing our prayers and our worship.

Every time we sing a song to the Lord, dance, draw a picture, or write a poem, our worship goes into one of those bowls and a wisp of aromatic smoke goes up before Him. Each prayer rises as fragrant incense. Our God is constantly smelling the soothing aroma of our worship.

My prayer: Let the offering of my life be sweet and soothing, a puff of beautifully pungent incense before You, God. Let it please Your heart and bring You pleasure.

In conclusion—did I enter in spirit, did I come in truth, did I open up my heart, did I encounter God, was I touched by His presence, am I leaving different than when I came? If so, then I have truly worshiped.

Selah – pause in His presence

·

Chapter 12

THE WARFARE OF WORSHIP

I would like us to pull up a chair on the front porch of our house of worship. Take a look around at the four supporting pillars—God's glory, His presence, His goodness, and the light of His countenance. Because of the brightness we carry, it's no secret that some of the most dangerous people to the devil are God's worshipers. He is also jealous of them because he used to have a major role in the worship ministry of heaven. For these reasons, he frequently attacks them out of bitterness and hatred.

I have lost many friends to the battle that surrounds worship. I honor those who have gone before me. They paid a price, some of them with their lives, paving the way for what I now carry. I have a dear friend, a worship leader, who died from cancer a few years ago. He wrote songs and worshiped until his last breath. He is now part of the cloud of witnesses cheering me on. There are many others—some young, some old, who have fought the same battle. This chapter is dedicated to them.

I have a clear image of a sermon I once heard on spiritual warfare. The speaker took an armchair, moved it to one side of the stage and sat down in it. He then popped up the foot rest, raised his hands toward heaven in a posture of worship, and said, "This is how I do spiritual warfare."

There are few things that confound the enemy like worship and praise. I will add a few other words to my torture list for the devil as well, things that go hand in hand with worship—rest, childlike faith, trust, hope, and quiet confidence.

Legal Challenges

A few years back, someone filed an action against me on an acreage that I owned. It was not due to anything I had done. The former owner of the property had done some shady things that I was unaware of before he sold it to me—and then, unfortunately, he died. By default, I found myself stuck in the middle of a very messy situation, one that was far beyond my ability to comprehend or sort out. The dollar figures associated with the accusations were enough to break me for years to come. I had no idea what to do.

As the weeks went on, depression and turmoil came against me. I constantly heard voices telling me that I would never recover from this, that I was trapped with no way out. I began to doubt God's leading for me to buy the property, and started to question my ability to hear His voice. My vision became dark and clouded.

One spring afternoon, I was home by myself. I decided to go outside onto the patio for a few minutes. The property was on a ravine with huge cedar trees lining the yard. A delicate breeze was coming up the valley, and the cherry tree in front of the house was in full bloom. The song birds were busy gathering small twigs for their nests, and the bees were buzzing around the flowers.

As I looked out at the stunning scene, tears came to my eyes and I found hope in the thought that if my heavenly Father cared for the birds, how much more would He care for me.

I gathered up enough spiritual strength to go down the stairs to the driveway which was narrow and windy—it was maybe eighty feet long, and it went up a hill. I lifted my hands toward heaven and started singing praise. At first my thoughts mocked me, but I continued on. As I walked up the

> *There are few things that confound the enemy like worship and praise*

driveway, I sang louder. Within a few minutes' time, I noticed the depression lifting off me. Once I got to the top of the driveway, I turned around and started coming down again; this time I began twirling and dancing.

Once at the bottom, I turned around and headed back up the driveway again. Now my song turned to one of joy. I sang, danced, twirled, jumped, and rejoiced all over that property—from one end to the other for over forty-five minutes that afternoon. When I finally went back in the house, I was completely out of breath and badly in need of a shower.

The following week, the legal action was dropped with absolutely no explanation. All of the threats and accusations disappeared in a matter of days and never returned. I eventually sold the property and it turned out to be a great source of blessing for me.

The Disappearing Flu

A while ago I caught a really bad winter flu. I don't often get sick but this one took me by surprise, and I went down hard. As my body cycled through a series of symptoms, I tried to stand on God's word when it came to my healing, but the situation got worse and ended up as a bronchial infection. By the fourth day, I was seriously ill.

That evening, I picked up my bible and attempted to read, but my eyes would hardly even focus on the page. I got up out of bed and stumbled into my study, almost too dizzy to even stand. With nothing left to lose, I determined to bring a sacrifice of praise over my situation—because no sickness can change the fact that He is still worthy to be worshiped.

I lifted my hands toward heaven and began slowly waving them around the room. I almost stumbled and fell, but I pressed on, offering up verbal thanksgiving and praise with as much strength as I had in me. In about two minutes, I noticed a shift as God's presence came into the room.

I persisted for a few minutes longer and suddenly noticed that I was starting to feel better. At this point in time, I began jumping up and down, dancing, and rejoicing. The more I worshiped, the stronger I felt. Symptoms began dropping off, dizziness left, and a massive headache started to fade away. By the next morning, the last of the bronchial infection had vacated my body and I was back to one hundred percent health wise.

Strange Lights

Several years ago, I ended up in a season of life that felt like the perfect storm. I had just been laid off from my job and was struggling to find purpose and direction in life. Along with that, we had just done a series of medical tests in order to renew our life insurance. While mine came back clear, my wife's came back with some concerns. Through a series of further examinations, we discovered something that the doctors told us was very likely cancer.

The following weeks were pure hell for me. There is nothing worse than playing a waiting game with test results and scans. I also kept running into people who either had cancer, or who had loved ones with it—even the same kind that we were faced with. With little for financial resources and a sick wife, once again, I felt the fingers of depression reaching into my soul.

Eventually an exploratory procedure was booked and we began the waiting game to find out the results. The night after the surgery, I remember sitting in my home office. My spirit was crushed and my emotions were oscillating between anger and despair. However, I decided to spend some time worshiping. With shaking hands and a trembling voice, I focused my eyes on heaven and started singing. As I did, I felt God's glory come and rest upon me. This gave me strength to press in further. I sang for more than an hour and then switched to praying in the spirit for a period of time.

My office was unique in that it had windows surrounding it on three sides. Looking out the windows, I could see that it was an overcast night with quite a bit of low cloud cover. As I stared blankly into the cloudy darkness, a sudden blinding light split the sky from horizon to horizon. Then a second light came, even brighter than the first one. The low clouds seemed to serve as giant reflectors for the lights, making them appear as if they filled up the whole sky. I didn't understand what had happened, but at that moment, I knew that God had received my worship and I was able to rest.

The next morning, I read in the news that two large meteorites had burned up in the atmosphere over our region at the exact time that I was worshiping.

> *Worship brings an alternate focus to our hearts and a stability to our thinking*

That same day, we got a call from the doctor's office with an appointment to go and view the results of the surgery. When we went in to the appointment the doctor came into the room with a huge smile on her face. She said that she didn't often get to bring good news to people, but our tests had come back absolutely clean—there was no cancer.

By the end of that same week, I had a meeting with someone who offered me a job and I started working shortly after.

Selah – pause in His presence

An Understated Weapon

Worship is a most powerful weapon. It cuts through every tactic that the enemy has at his disposal. Where he brings confusion, worship brings rest. Where he brings depression, worship renews hope. Where the enemy brings words of despair, worship brings peace and confidence.

Worship brings an alternate focus to our hearts and a stability to our thinking. It is part of the process of renewing our mind. Imagine the devil trying for months to instill fear and hopelessness over a situation. Then think of the power of worship dismantling all of the prison walls and lies in a matter of a few minutes. The devil is no match for a person of the presence—one who chooses to worship in every circumstance.

The devil is a being of finite resources. There is a fire in his soul that is decimating him from the inside out—he does not have unlimited power. From the moment that he attacks us, his candle begins to burn down. The only thing that brings fuel to his fire is our agreement with his lies. Jesus said it plainly, *"He is a liar and the father of lies."* He has only one thing in his arsenal: the power of deception.

Spirit and truth worship tears down lies. It also helps focus our attention, bringing us the perspectives of heaven. When we worship, we are infused with glory. We are strengthened and renewed. While the devil's candle burns down, the light in our heart *"Shines ever brighter until the full light of day."* (Proverbs 4:18)

Angels

Angels love to worship God, but they are also inspired by our worship. Their worship comes from a slightly different perspective than ours—their world being filled with the constant light and glory of heaven. When we bow down and give praise in the middle of dark and troubling circumstances, they can't help but be attracted to the scene. They become active and powerful agents in the quest of God's people when true worship is on display.

There are many examples in the bible of battles being won from a position of worship.

Joshua

Joshua was faced with a difficult battle against the Amalekites. As he and the Israelites fought down in the valley, Moses went up on a mountain and raised his hands toward heaven in a posture of worship and intercession.

> *It turned out that whenever Moses raised his hands, Israel was winning, but whenever he lowered his hands, Amalek was winning. But Moses' hands got tired. So they got a stone and set it under him. He sat on it and Aaron and Hur held up his hands, one on each side. So his hands remained steady until the sun went down. Joshua defeated Amalek and its army in battle.*

(Exodus 17:11-13 MES)

On another occasion, Joshua was getting ready to go up against Jericho—a very strong, walled city. The evening before the battle, he had an encounter that included worship and an angel.

> *While Joshua was there near Jericho, He looked up and saw right in front of him a man standing, holding his drawn sword. Joshua stepped up to him and said, "Whose side are you on— ours or our enemies'?" He said, "Neither. I'm commander of God's army. I've just arrived." Joshua fell, face to the*

ground, and worshiped. He asked, "What orders does my Master have for his servant?"

(Joshua 5:13-14 MES)

The angel gave Joshua a battle strategy that was crazy brilliant. They were to march around the perimeter of the city for seven days while carrying the ark of the covenant— God's presence. Then on the seventh day, they were to march seven times around the city and at the sound of the trumpets give a loud shout of praise. The force of the worship of God's people flattened the walls of the city, and a great victory was won.

Worship - Confusing to the Enemy

Worship brings the focus of our eyes onto heaven. In the middle of a dark situation, this brings a great deal of confusion to the enemy. He has little ability to make sense of praise offered in this setting.

The evening before a battle that should have been an easy victory for the enemy, Gideon bowed down in worship before his God. A few hours later, Gideon and three hundred men armed with clay jars, candles, and trumpets, defeated a vast and well-equipped Midianite army. For the most part, the adversary fell into disarray and started killing each other.

The same thing happened with Jehoshaphat when faced with a powerful enemy. After holding a massive worship gathering, he sent the Levite worshipers out in front of his army. This was the word of the Lord, spoken through the prophets.

You will not need to fight in this battle. Position yourselves, stand still and see the salvation of the Lord, who is with you.

(1 Chronicles 20:17 NKJV)

The next day, God sent ambushes against the enemy. After running around in chaos for a while, they turned on each other in confusion and destroyed themselves.

Samuel Brings Thunder

Samuel was a seer, a prophet, and an extreme worshiper. He was the last judge of Israel and he mentored a young man, David, who eventually became king. Throughout Samuel's life, the Israelites were constantly at war with the Philistines. During one of these wars, Samuel decided to worship.

So Samuel took a young lamb and offered it to the Lord as a whole burnt offering. He pleaded with the Lord to help Israel, and the Lord answered him. Just as Samuel was sacrificing the burnt offering, the Philistines arrived to attack Israel. But the Lord spoke with a mighty voice of thunder from heaven that day, and the Philistines were thrown into such confusion that the Israelites defeated them.

(1 Samuel 7:9-10)

David

David was another warrior who experienced breakthroughs as a worshiper. He dealt with battles on many different levels. As a young, anointed musician, David was called to the palace to play music in front of king Saul, a man who had mental illness issues complicated by evil spirit oppression. Whenever the evil spirit came to trouble Saul, David played his harp. The presence of God, released from David's worship would drive the demonic oppression away from Saul.

No evil presence can persist in an atmosphere of worship. There have been many times that I have sensed various demonic forces and powers of darkness along my journey. My response is not to start yelling, screaming, or rebuking. Instead, I have learned to worship. As I focus on heaven, I have found that the enemy leaves quickly.

David wrote some beautiful words in the twenty-third psalm, *"You prepare a feast for me in the presence of my enemies."* The devil doesn't have the stomach to watch a banquet where the great Shepherd loves on His people. I have heard it said that when we worship, Jesus puts it on the devil's loudspeaker. He loves to put us in view, but out of reach of the enemy.

Right before David became king, he found himself in a situation where all of the families of his army were taken off to captivity and their homes were destroyed and burned. David's men were so despondent that they talked of stoning him, but David *"Encouraged himself in the Lord."* (1 Samuel 30:6) I imagine David taking his harp and lifting his

> *As we learn to focus on heaven, the enemy will leave quickly*

song of praise before the Lord God. After consulting with the priest, David and a small group of men went out and recovered everything that had been stolen from them—not one person was lost. Two weeks later, David was crowned as king of Israel.

Psalms

There are many psalms that speak about bringing praise in the middle of dreadful circumstances.

Psalm 8 is sometimes called the "psalm of the astronomer." It speaks of childlike praise and worship silencing enemies and building strongholds of safety.

> *You have built a stronghold by the songs of babies. Strength rises up with the chorus of singing children. This kind of praise has the power to shut Satan's mouth. Childlike worship will silence the madness of those who oppose you.*

(Psalm 8:2 TPT)

In Psalm 27, David is found worshiping while his enemies surround him.

> *Then I will hold my head high above my enemies who surround me. At his sanctuary I will offer sacrifices with shouts of joy, singing and praising the Lord with music.*

(Psalm 27:6)

Psalm 149 is a psalm of praise written by an unknown author. It begins with a celebration. Here are some words used in the first few verses of this poem: praising, singing, rejoicing, dancing, making melody, and playing tambourines and lyres. Then it describes what happens when we worship—read this slowly and carefully.

Childlike praise and worship silences the enemy and builds a stronghold of safety

Godly lovers triumph in the glory of God, and their joyful praises will rise even while others sleep. God's high and holy praises fill their mouths, for their shouted praises are their weapons of war! These warring weapons will bring vengeance on every opposing force and every resistant power—to bind kings with chains and rulers with iron shackles. Praise-filled warriors will enforce the judgment-doom decreed against their enemies. This is the glorious honor he gives to all his godly lovers. Hallelujah! Praise the Lord!

(Psalm 149:5-9 TPT)

Paul and Silas

Paul and Silas were preaching in the city of Philippi when they were confronted by a demonized slave girl with a gift of fortune telling. She followed them around for several days until Paul finally became annoyed and cast the demon out of her. Once the demon was gone, her gift of fortune telling also left and her owners became very angry.

They caused such an uproar in the city that Paul and Silas were dragged before the magistrate who had them severely beaten with rods. They were thrown into prison with their feet fastened in stocks.

Around midnight Paul and Silas were praying and singing hymns to God, and the other prisoners were listening. Suddenly, there was a massive earthquake, and the prison was shaken to its foundations. All the doors immediately flew open, and the chains of every prisoner fell off!

(Acts 16:25-26)

As a result of this event, a great revival broke out in Philippi. It started with the prison guard. He and his family got saved and baptized that night before dawn even broke.

Without Agenda

Worship is not a battle strategy. It is not something that we can use to our advantage to get out of a tough situation. In the breakthroughs that have come to me through worship and praise, I have brought my offerings for one reason—because He is worthy. It doesn't matter what is happening around us, nothing can ever change that fact. Worship must be without agenda. God will not be manipulated through praise. He also will not stand by idle as one of His children brings an offering before Him, in spirit and truth, in a dark time.

I have learned that regardless of the end result, worship is never the wrong thing to do. Even if nothing seems to happen, God is still worthy to be glorified. What might look like a lost battle from an earthly perspective is nothing more than a seed for an even greater breakthrough—either for yourself, or for another person as they pick up the mantle of praise that has been left behind.

Perhaps the most awesome part of a battle won through singing a song, painting a picture, or dancing on a driveway is the fact that when God is done doing all the fighting, He leans over to us with a big smile and whispers "Well done! You really thrashed the enemy this time!" In that moment, we get to turn around and give Him all the glory!

So the next time you are faced with a battle, do something drastic. Go and find your armchair!

Selah – pause in His presence

ENCOUNTERED *in* WORSHIP

Chapter 13

WORSHIP AS A LIFESTYLE

In this chapter, we are going to take worship out of the house and into the streets. "In spirit and truth" worship is portable. It doesn't matter where we are—at home, at work, in a dungeon, in a palace, Hawaii (yay!), Nepal, in an airplane—on a boat, with a goat, in a box, with a fox, here or there, ANYWHERE! (*Green Eggs and Ham* memories momentarily surfacing), we can always worship.

Worship is a two-sided coin. It can be offered individually and at corporate gatherings. It can also be expressed as a lifestyle. One is not complete without the other.

> *Dear brothers and sisters, I plead with you to give your bodies to God because of all he has done for you. Let them be a living and holy sacrifice—the kind he will find acceptable. This is truly the way to worship him. Don't copy the behavior and customs of this world, but let God transform you into a new person*

by changing the way you think. Then you will learn to know God's will for you, which is good and pleasing and perfect.

(Romans 12:1-2)

The word "worship" in this verse is the Greek word "Latreuo." It mirrors the Hebrew word "Avodah" which means work, worship, and service. The entire scope of our lives can be a seamless flow of worship before the Lord.

24/7 Worship

And you shall love the Lord your God with all your heart, and with all your soul, and with all your mind, and with all your strength.

(Mark 12:30 NASB)

It is stunning to think that everything we do—our thoughts, our actions, our work, our play, and our relationships could be offered up to the Lord as worship. We don't have a well-developed framework for this type of worship today, but to the ancient Jewish sages it was an essential part of life—interwoven into the very fiber of their culture. These people understood instinctively how to live out a 24/7 worship lifestyle before the Lord.

Although worship was celebrated in every area of life, the realm of work was particularly holy before the Lord. Even to this day, an orthodox Jewish person considers their work as an offering of worship to Jehovah. I believe this is the reason why the Jewish people are known for prosperity, creativity, and ingenuity.

I did a recent search of the inventions and innovations brought to our world by the Jewish race. In all areas—from scientific, to medical, to technological and beyond, these people have blessed our world with more creative solutions to major world problems than any other people group. Without doubt, this is a direct result of their historical embrace of latreuo/avodah worship.

Much of my life experience has been dedicated to the gathering together of God's people in corporate worship settings. Only in the past few years have I started to grasp what it might look like to worship God with everything I do. Here are a few observations that have come out of my heart as I have desired to encounter God in an "Avodah worship lifestyle."

Awareness is Everything

I believe that a large part of this journey is awareness. If I am mindful of the possibilities, I am more given to an attitude of worship throughout the day. I have also found that if I offer every moment to God as an act of worship, I become conscious of His presence in all of my activities. I have only experienced the tip of this iceberg, but as I

> *Everything we do can be offered up to the Lord as worship*

climb higher, a great anticipation has started to rise in my heart. I now believe it is possible to live with a constant awareness of the presence of God—the fire of God's glory continually stoked on the altar of my life.

I am also learning to make an equal sacrifice in both good and bad times. If I have a heart full of thanksgiving, praise, and worship when everything is going well, and then stop the flow when things go badly, I find it difficult to return to a place of worship again. Since there is no way to selectively numb emotions, I am determined to offer up all ends of the spectrum as worship.

There is a place of consistency that comes with a full surrender to an Avodah lifestyle. Once I am restfully centered, it is much easier to ride the wave of the Spirit of God, soaring above the many troubling situations that come across my path. I am able to hear the voice of the Holy Spirit on a steady basis and a realm of favor opens up before me like an unfolding

> *I have discovered a world of creativity as I have learned to open up my life as a constant sacrifice*

pathway. I find myself in the center of the will of God—constantly in the right place at the right time. When I lose my focus, I hear very little from God and the favor seems somewhat dampened.

I have also discovered a world of creativity as I have learned to open up my life as a constant sacrifice. Inspired ideas come to me and innovative solutions are downloaded into my mind and heart. Often, they don't even have any spiritual content and are extremely practical.

Encounters with Avodah

Recently I was in the process of figuring out how to best renovate my kitchen. I had asked God for wisdom on how to best lay out the floor plan, but I was a bit stumped. One day I was at work, joyfully offering up my life and singing praises under my breath, when the entire plan was suddenly impressed on my spirit. I am always taken aback by these moments—they constantly surprise me.

> *Let's take our place outside with Jesus, no longer pouring out the sacrificial blood of animals but pouring out sacrificial praises from our lips to God in Jesus' name. Make sure you don't take things for granted and go slack in working for the common good; share what you have with others. God takes particular pleasure in acts of worship—a different kind of "sacrifice"—that take place in the kitchen and workplace and on the streets.*

(Hebrews 13:14-15 MES)

A few months ago, I was helping to assemble a building. The guys on the site were stereotypical construction workers—they were constantly swearing, telling off-color jokes, and making dishonoring comments about women. As I worked with them for two days, I prayed in the spirit under my breath and did my best to serve the overall progress of the job. I didn't say anything negative to them or express my disgust at their language choices. I simply focused on hosting God's presence and carried out my duties to the best of my abilities.

By late in the first afternoon, I noticed that they weren't swearing anymore. The next morning, they began coming to me when decisions needed to be made, looking to me for advice and leadership. At the end of the day, a group of them came up to me and said, "It has been such a privilege working with you for the past two days." I wished them well and pronounced a blessing over their lives—something they didn't even realize I was doing. As I left the job site, I prayed over their vehicles, asking God to encounter them and bring others into their lives to water the seeds of His presence that had been planted.

It's Electric!

I have a friend who is an electrician. He is a crazy worshiper and a person of the presence. He often finds that people on his job sites check their language for no apparent reason when he is around. Someone recently asked why he didn't talk negatively about his wife like the rest of the work crew. People he is working with feel safe around him, frequently sharing sensitive details of their lives without any prompting.

One day, as he was working, one of his colleagues began to randomly open up to him—telling about the psychologists he had seen and the deep secrets of his struggles against depression. He then stopped himself and said, "I have no idea why I am telling you this right now." When you carry God's presence and worship as a priority, anything can happen!

> *Our bodies are living, holy, and acceptable in God's sight*

Sometimes, my friend will take his guitar out to the park, sit on a park bench and sing songs to the Lord. On one occasion, someone was riding by on a bike with headphones on and music blaring, but something in the atmosphere grabbed the cyclist's attention. After doing a hard 180 degree turn around, he rode right up to my friend as he sang. Tears filled his eyes as he took his headphones off and listened intently for a few minutes. When the song ended, he said, "You have no idea how much I needed that today."

At a Bus Stop?

I have another longtime acquaintance who is an insurance adjuster. He is in the habit of getting up early, listening to his favorite bible teachers, and then taking the bus to work with the presence of the Holy Spirit resting on him. One morning, he was waiting at the bus stop when a total stranger sat down beside him and blurted out, "Tell me what it's like to be born again!" After talking to the individual for a few short minutes about Jesus, the bus pulled up and my friend headed off to work.

A Suitable Offering

It is no coincidence that Jesus offered up His body in the ultimate sacrifice on the cross, and it is our bodies that God wants us to present to Him as a continuous sacrifice of worship. Our bodies are living, holy, and acceptable in God's sight. They are His temple and He has put His glory inside of us.

Speaking specifically of work, each of us has been given a skill set—a combination of natural dispositions and mental capacities. The blend of our bodies and our minds is what we use to make a living. As we go about our business, it is possible to constantly direct our activities toward heaven as worship.

As this offering rises before God, His presence settles on our day. The process of transformation through grace begins to take hold of our lives, and our minds become renewed. We start to think differently. This sets us up for the will of God to be established in our lives—those things good, pleasing, and perfect.

A Prophetic Picture

I have a dear friend who had a prophetic vision a few years ago. She was at home spending time in the presence of God, worshiping with music in the background. In an instant, her eyes were opened up to the world of the spirit, and she saw what was happening as she worshiped. Every time a key was played on an instrument, a string was plucked on a guitar, a stick was hit on a drum, or a word was sung, it would rise as an animated music note. An angel would then grab the stem of the note and rush off to an unknown location in the world to do warfare. There were thousands of notes rising from each song, every detail being captured by myriads of angels.

Selah – pause in His presence

Just Imagine

Our world is a broken place. The curse, released when we humans turned against God, has left humankind in a constant state of panic and fear. Everywhere we turn, there is a tragic situation, a problem to be solved, a financial crisis, or an injustice staring us in the face. A constant cry goes up for answers to difficult questions in our world.

For this reason, God has strategically placed His worshipers all over the earth. They are in every nation and city. They hold positions in governments, on boards, and in societies. The work in every type of vocation that exists—they cut hair, run businesses, and work in the service industry. They are teachers in schools and colleges. They are moms, dads, children, and grandparents.

I would like us to dream together. Imagine what it would look like if each believer, worldwide, learned to offer his or her every moment to God as worship. Think of ten thousands of angels, surrounding the people of God, capturing every word of praise, every prayer offered under a breath, every smile offered to someone in turmoil, every random act of kindness.

Think of the people of God—millions of them all over the earth—working at their jobs, going above and beyond the call of duty, offering it all up as worship before the throne. What would happen if we preferred others above ourselves or went the extra mile to help someone in need? Every one of these offerings is an act of worship. With each sacrifice,

> *God has strategically placed His worshipers all over the earth*

the incense rises, creating an opening for the kingdom of God to be established here on earth as it is in heaven.

Worship Brings Healing

Hundreds of diseases constantly afflict our world for which there are no medical solutions. What would it look like if we, as God's people, began worshiping over our medical centers, our nursing homes, and the research labs of the world? Imagine a world where unprecedented medical breakthroughs came about because of a constant stream of worship directed toward heaven—the angels catching the wind of every sacrifice and using it to defeat sickness. What would it look like if entire hospitals and critical illness wards were closed down because there weren't enough patients to fill them?

Worship Brings Peace

If there is one thing that is elusive in our world, it is peace on every level of human existence. What would happen if every breath we are given was exhaled as worship, releasing the "shalom" of heaven over our planet? Imagine the impact of peace on the starving populations of our war-torn world. Much of the devastation we experience on an international level has been caused by war and violence. Heaven's peace leaves a much different looking wake, one of wholeness and contentment—nothing missing and nothing broken.

> *What would innovative solutions look like in the places where God has given you influence?*

Worship Brings Hope

As I look into the eyes of many around me, I see an empty hopelessness. Depression is rampant everywhere I go. What would hope look like, shining through the darkness like a ray of light, all because hopeful people choose to worship? Imagine a world free from antidepressants—where depression is defeated over entire regions and cities. What would empty mental health hospitals look like?

Worship Unleashes Creativity

When I sit in board room meetings, I am constantly stirred by the need for wisdom. Creative solutions are lacking in every corner of our society. Worship brings with it the ability to tap into the creative vault of heaven. With Avodah worship on the hearts of God's people, I dream of breakthroughs and transformation in our workplaces, regions, cities, and countries.

There are practical solutions and a world of inspired ideas in a lifestyle of worship. What would innovative solutions look like in the places where God has given *you* influence? Can you dare to believe that they might be poured out through your life? Dream! Worship! With the creativity of heaven unleashed on the earth, our world would surely not look the same.

Worship Brings Freedom from Fear

I have noticed something consistent in the people around me—they are afraid. They hide from their past, cower in the present, and are terrified of the future. They fear sickness, financial loss, and natural disasters. God's worshipers carry the answer. We have not been given a spirit of fear but of power, love, and a sound mind. Fear is a demonic spirit that cannot stand in the pathway of worship. What would it look like for an entire people group to live without fear, reacting with faith and love to everything that comes their way? With all of God's people worshiping with their heart, soul, mind, and strength, it is entirely possible!

Worship Changes the Atmosphere

As we worship, the presence and glory of Jesus invades the earth. From the perspective of the powers of darkness, this is a violent act. From the viewpoint of heaven, the invasion looks like rest. Worship is an atmosphere changer. With the glory of God hovering over a region, chains are broken off people in every area of culture. What would it look like for the devouring power of restlessness to be broken? In place of a shattered self-image, what would new confidence look like? What if broken relationships were restored and lost hearts began to search for faith?

The answers to the problems of our world are found in the massive heart of God. As we offer our lives in worship, they are revealed to us by His Spirit. There is no problem too difficult for God. We, His people, carry the keys and the answers to every difficult situation that exists.

> *For as the waters fill the sea, the earth will be filled with an awareness of the glory of the Lord.*

(Habakkuk 2:14)

Imagine the glory of God that would hover over the earth, if all of God's people began to worship—every day, all day, and all night! Our world would be forever changed, transformed, and renewed by the presence of God released upon His people.

They worshiped without ceasing, day and night, singing, "Holy, holy, holy is the Lord God, the Almighty! The Was, the Is, and the Coming!"

(Revelation 4:8 TPT)

I will leave you dreaming of this type of open-heaven environment over your city, and I will dream of the same over mine.

Selah – pause in His presence

ENCOUNTERED *in* WORSHIP

Chapter 14

INTIMATE WORSHIP

(with Misty Bedwell & Carolyn Joy Currey)

God is a being of extreme love. He also has a sensitive heart. I have a friend who had a recent encounter with heaven where she was lifted up onto the Father's lap. As she sat there, fingers curled up in the edge of His robe, she noticed something unusual. With as big as God was, she thought His skin would be thick and strong; however, she found that it was very delicate and soft. It was so thin that she could see right through into His heart, which was also transparent. She knew that she could have easily hurt Him.

God has made Himself vulnerable to His children and their worship. When we worship Him in spirit and truth, it touches His heart to a degree for which we have no understanding. It returns to Him what He has so freely given to us—His glory. I have a world full of awe for a God who has made Himself open and accessible to us in this way.

Much of this book has focused on worship as it relates to our Father God. We have entered the throne room, knelt in

His presence, cast our crowns at His feet, and gazed at His radiant glory.

The heart of God, revealed to us in Jesus, contains another side of worship—a story so rich in beauty and imagery that it almost defies description. Jesus has also made Himself vulnerable to our worship.

There is a grand, eternal romance between Jesus and His bride with worship as its centerpiece. The great mystery of heaven is found in how Jesus is smitten by our worship—we are the object of His desire. We are living this love story now, and we will be wrapped up in it for eternity.

> *Standing beside you, glistening in your pure and golden glory, is the beautiful bride-to-be! Now listen, daughter, pay attention, and forget about your past. For your royal Bridegroom is ravished by your beautiful brightness. Bow in reverence before him, for he is your Lord!*

(Psalm 45:9,11 TPT)

There is something captivating in the thought that Jesus' love for us is so complete, we can safely let go of everything in our past. Once we have experienced this kind of intimacy, things behind us hold very little meaning. We have been given a new beginning through His blood. He has paid the price for our past to be erased and forgotten. He has chosen us as His royal bride!

The Royal Garden

I would like for us to step outside the door of our house of worship. Walk around the side, and look toward the back yard. With the eyes of your heart, you will find a garden that stretches out for eternity. The garden has a name—Eden, an ancient Hebrew word that means "pleasure and delight." As humans, our journey started in a place of intimacy, creativity, peace, joy, love, and connection. This is *our* garden, but it is also *your* garden. Each and every person has a personally designed version of Eden in his or her heart.

> *For the Lord comforts Zion; He comforts all her waste places and makes her wilderness like Eden, her desert like the garden of the Lord; joy and gladness will be found in her, thanksgiving and the voice of song.*

(Isaiah 51:3 ESV)

As a worshiping community, we have been brought back to Zion, to the place where worship all started, to the mountain called Moriah where Abraham sacrificed Isaac, to the place of David's humble ark-tent. Does it feel like you have a wilderness inside of you? How about a desert? With full surrender to intimate garden worship, those dry places can be restored to a place

> *Jesus' love for us is so complete, we can safely let go of everything in our past*

of beauty and rest once again. Eden looks like joy and gladness, feels like thanksgiving, and sounds like music and celebration.

We are going to explore what worship is like in the setting of the garden of the Lord. I have walked in this royal garden many times, but I am not going to describe it on my own. I have asked a couple of friends to help me put into words what their version of the garden looks like, and what worship is like when they are there.

Misty Bedwell is a visual artist, a writer, and a person who has the ability to lead worship in many different ways—whether it be with a paint brush, a song, or an outside-the-box presentation to a group of people. Carolyn Currey is a professional dancer and choreographer, a creative storyteller, and an author. Yet if you were to ask either of them *who* they are, I know they wouldn't want to be described by what they do. They would both want to be known as daughters of the Father and lovers of Jesus.

These two crazy worshipers are dear sisters to me. Together, we are founders of an organization called Creative Launch, a school of worship dedicated to mentoring creative worshipers into artistic expression and freedom. Their input in this chapter is highly valued and greatly appreciated.

What does the garden look like, smell like, sound like?

Dean - The garden is a place of peace. Upon entering it, I find a cascading fountain filled with the water of life, and a simple bench off to the side. The tree of life is located at its center. Crisscrossing the garden is a labyrinth of paths that lead in different directions. The paths are cut out of what almost seems like a transparent golden granite material.

One time I decided to take a closer look at the detail of the paving stones. I discovered that there, inscribed in the walkways, was God's love written over me. It described me in thousands of unique and beautiful ways and was engraved in what appeared to be several miles of walkways. For the first time, I understood the verse, *"How precious are your thoughts about me O God. I can't even count them; they outnumber the grains of sand!"* (Psalm 139:17-18)

Jesus meets me in the garden and it is also a place where I go just to be alone. It is saturated with His presence, the sound of water, and the pungent fragrance of springtime. There are royal trees, flowerbeds, and lush grassy areas. There is a river that runs beside it, but you have to take a pathway through a grove of trees to get there.

Misty - I only see His feet, and often don't notice my surroundings. There is an urgency inside me to keep up to His pace as He walks. I don't want to miss out on anything; I must stay close. Many times, I have had to retrace my steps because He turned the corner, and the branches filled in the narrow path.

He is my garden, my rose, my fountain. I can smell His skin, see the impressions in the soil under His feet, touch the hem of His garment. Sometimes I cling on for the ride, never once slowing Him down. And when He stops, I am filled with anticipation as we wait together. Where are we now? Have we arrived or are we just resting? How long will we stay? In these moments, I often close my eyes so I can see.

Carolyn - As a child, I dreamed of this garden. I wandered under a rose trellis and entered an inner sanctuary that was incredibly green and quiet. To my left, Jesus sat on a simple bench and smiled in welcome. I sat on the ground close to Him and laid my head on His lap. I couldn't imagine wanting anything else. The peace and safety didn't just exist in that place, somehow it soaked into my heart so I could carry it with me. I was only eleven years old, with no idea of what life would hold for me, but somehow I grasped the deep treasure of the moment. I wanted it to last forever.

As though He read my mind, Jesus told me I could come back to this place anytime I wanted for the rest of my life. I had no concept how much I would need that place of rest and refuge, but I just believed Him. Since then, the garden with His close presence has always been there.

There is an extra joy that comes with inviting others to it now. They don't come with me—the place of intimacy is only for two. But I can point: "There's the rose trellis. Go see what's inside."

How do we enter the garden, how does Jesus enter our garden, how do we meet him there?

My bridegroom-king has a vineyard of love made from a multitude of followers. His caretakers of this vineyard have given my beloved their best. But as for my own vineyard of love, I give it all to you forever. My beloved, one with me in my garden, how marvelous that my friends, the brides-to-be, now hear your voice and song. Let me now hear it again.

(Song of Songs 8:11,13 TPT)

Dean - Entering the garden takes faith. I have to believe that I am invited there and that I am experiencing something that is real. Often, I will give thanks and praise until the earth starts to fade away.

Where I find myself in the garden is always a surprise. It could be in any number of places—on a bench, up in a tree, on top of a rock, or off in a corner. If I listen, I will hear Jesus calling me closer. Sometimes He is there waiting; sometimes I will go looking for Him.

Jesus is very spontaneous and likes surprises. He is also one of the funniest people I know, full of laughter and wit. If I am not careful, He will take the opportunity to startle me from behind a rock or a tree. He also might appear in a costume of some kind—predictability is not an option when Jesus is around.

Misty - He is always available although I do not always see Him. When I believe what He said in His word, faith rises up in me and my ability to connect with Him gets clearer, easier, more tangible. In the heat of an afternoon, a breeze will come and wrap itself around me, bringing with it the promise of His presence. When I believe, the eyes of my heart are opened, and I know He is near.

Carolyn - Entering the garden always looks like believing I will not be alone there. Sometimes it means quietly entering to wait—all the while aware that I'm being observed with love from some place I cannot see. If the wait is long, there may be something to notice in the meantime, and He will want to hear what I thought of it when He chooses to be seen. He will have something profound to share about it too.

When He enters it's always with joy and the mutual laughter of satisfied anticipation. When He is there first, there is a welcome waiting for me. It is wrapped in wonder for all He is. Sometimes He is seen in a cloud, sometimes in a fire of glory.

What does worship look like in the garden?

Dean - Worship in the garden is a deeply moving encounter. There is worship that is filled with awe and sacrifice, but garden worship is an experience of sharing love. It is the fruit of the tree of life. I find that when I pour out my love on Him, love is returned back into my soul. I have discovered that glory looks like love in the garden. The result is always a full surrender to His love and a transformation of who I am—I never leave this place of worship the same as when I came.

Misty - Worship in this place never looks the same. When I follow the pathway to the garden to worship, there is always an invitation to abandon my pride. I will often find myself creating new movements, utilizing crazy colorful brush strokes, and discovering the edges of my emotions in my bare feet. I become lost in the smell of honey, in His reassurance, in remembering the things He's said. Nothing else matters in those moments. Everything pales in comparison with who He is—there are no concerns greater than His name. I leave with the eager anticipation of returning soon.

Carolyn – His heart is a treasure to be discovered, but like any relationship, it requires sensitivity. If I am quiet and look for His heart, I discover how to worship Him in a way that brings Him joy. Because He is a living being, this changes and shifts, which means I get to keep asking, keep seeking, keep connecting, and pursuing. In the end, the surprise is always that He was actually the one who was pursuing me.

The best moments are those when my plans are set aside in favor of responding to His call of intimacy. Worship may be enjoying a sunrise with Him that few others will see because it's too early. It may be playing tag with the lion when He appears. It is always self poured out—the willingness to be fully seen, and to return love fully.

What is intimacy in worship, what does it mean to be "one" with Him?

And I ask not only for these disciples, but also for all those who will one day believe in me through their message. I pray for them all to be joined together as one even as you and I, Father, are joined together as one. I pray for them to become one with us so that the world will recognize that you sent me.

(John 17:20-23)

Dean - Intimate worship is a response to love. It looks like being wrapped up in His presence to the point where He is lost in me and I become lost in Him—until there seems to be little difference between the two. Worship in this setting feels like being overwhelmed by goodness, overcome by love, caught up in delight, lost for words, fueled by fire, fully surrendered, taken apart and then put back together again—but differently.

Misty - Whatever I gaze at consumes my attention. When I begin to focus only on Him, there are moments when everything shifts and I wonder if I am inside of Him looking out His eyes. I can't always tell where He ends and I begin. It could be that I have lost myself or found Him entirely. "Abiding in Him," (John 15) is the phrase that brings the clearest meaning to this picture. Recognizing that He also abides in me is mind blowing. Sometimes I try to picture it. Everything else falls away.

Carolyn - He loves process for some reason. Being one with Him is a continual journey but the point is gazing at His face. When our attention is fixed on Him, we are likely to not even notice the change occurring in us.

It begins with an awareness of His presence as it enters and fills. I discover what His emotions are and lose myself in response to that. Sometimes it is like standing in the center of a flame. It is always mutual delight.

Living in two worlds may sometimes confuse others. I once had a dream that illustrated this so well. I was being tightly hugged by Jesus, but when someone walked past, they said, "That's really weird. It looks like you're hugging someone." I realized they couldn't see Jesus. My position of resting in an embrace would have looked very strange without being able to see the other One involved! There will be times when unity won't be understood by others because they can't see the whole picture. Don't move from the embrace. Curiosity allows for the possibility of exploration.

The kingdom of heaven is given to the children. Living in intimacy is possible when we approach worship like a child—because children are shamelessly intimate. There is always more. The childlike anticipation of deeper, fuller, and higher will never stop growing for all of eternity.

An Encounter with the Bridegroom

Let us rejoice and exalt him and give him glory, because the wedding celebration of the Lamb has come. And his bride has made herself ready. Fine linen, shining bright and clear, has been given to her to wear, and the fine linen represents the righteous deeds of his holy believers.

(Revelation 19:7-10)

One morning, a few years ago, I woke up early and decided to spend some time worshiping before starting my day.

I picked up my guitar and began to sing, making up spontaneous songs as I often do, but there was something unusual in the air—it was as if Jesus was standing right in front of me. I pressed into worshiping Him with all my heart and as I did, His glory began radiating with an almost giddy excitement.

After a short while, His joy was so contagious that I stopped what I was doing and said, "What's up with you today? Why so excited?" He leaned in close to me and with an unmistakable voice said, "Do you remember what it was like in the days just before you were going to be married? I am getting married soon! The Father promised Me a bride as part of the reward for My suffering, and I have been waiting for her for centuries. Our wedding

> *I have come to discover that the purest motivation for worship is love*

is just a short time away. I love her with all My heart. She is so beautiful and I can hardly wait to spend the rest of My life with her."

Selah – pause in His presence

I have come to discover that the purest motivation for worship is love. Our love, expressed as the offering of our lives in intimate worship, brings Jesus to a place of a ravished heart.

These beautiful words, written in the Song of Songs, are simply outside the realm of understanding for me:

> *With one flash of your eyes I am undone by your love, my beloved, my equal, my bride. You leave me breathless—I am overcome by merely a glance from your worshiping eyes, for you have stolen my heart.*

> *Turn your eyes from me; I can't take it anymore! I can't resist the passion of these eyes that I adore. Overpowered by a glance, my ravished heart—undone. Held captive by your love, I am truly overcome! For your undying devotion to me is the most yielded sacrifice.*

(Song of Songs 4:9, 6:5 TPT)

I remember standing at the altar on the day my bride walked down the aisle toward me. When she got to the front of our little country church, the first thing I did was lift her veil.

Now we, as the bride of Christ, stand in front of Him. As we surrender to His gentle nail-scarred hands, He lifts our veil in His presence. We are set free to gaze into His face as

His glory light shines into our hearts. Our response can only be one thing—to worship Him.

Heaven looks like Jesus and His bride united for eternity. This stunning image has ramifications beyond comprehension. What does earthly intimacy look like translated into the spirit realm? What does raising children and creating family look like in paradise? Why would the eternal model of marriage and romance look like anything other than the perfect version of what God has given us here on this earth?

At the center of all things, worship will remain as the foundation of everything that binds us together with Him— the sharing of glory, the joy of being fully alive in Christ, and the consuming fire of His passion over us.

With these thoughts, our worship journey comes to an end—only to be continued forever. We are, without doubt, in for a future beyond our wildest imagination. But why wait? Why not start now? The kingdom of God is at hand. Let it be on earth as it is in heaven!

Selah – pause in His presence

ABOUT THE AUTHOR

Dean Maerz grew up in a small farming community on the Canadian prairies. He is a musician, mentor, teacher, writer, and blogger with a lifetime's worth of experience in music and worship as well as a passion for the presence of God. Dean and his wife currently reside in the Fraser Valley of Vancouver, BC, where Dean aspires to serve others well and worship his way through life.

For more information, other books written by Dean, and blog articles, go to:

www.presencenotes.com

CREATIVE LAUNCH

Creative Launch is a Worship Arts Mentorship Program located in the Fraser Valley area of Vancouver, Canada. It is designed to lead students into a deeper connection with God by exploring the Bible, worshiping with creative expression, collaboration in a mixed arts setting, and mentorship.

Content focus includes the following:

- Guidance for unique challenges specific to creative personalities.

- Techniques for shifting culture by refreshing faith, hope, and love.

- Strengthening identity in Christ through *fully alive* worship and prayer.

- Spiritual intimacy with Christ through exploration and Bible application.

- Creative arts focus—dance, art, music, and writing, and more.

- Courage mapping through "pleasantly disorienting" activities designed to push through fear, expand boundaries, and give back to the community.

- Exploration through group conversation, creative challenges, growth opportunities, and honest debriefing.

If you are a dancer, artist, musician, or writer looking for a place to be known and mentored, check us out at:

www.mycreativelaunch.com

on Facebook at: https://www.facebook.com/mycreativelaunch

on Instagram at: https://www.instagram.com/creative.launch

cl CREATIVE LAUNCH

Made in the USA
Columbia, SC
25 September 2020